W9-DJI-111

MAKE LOVE

notes on a
response-centered
curriculum

EDITED BY ALAN C. PURVES
University of Illinois

Contributing authors

WALLACE W. DOUGLAS

JAMES HOETKER

DELORES MINOR

SISTER MARY OWEN, S.N.D.

ROBERT D. ROBINSON

BARBARA TAYLOR

JERRY L. WALKER

ROBERT WEINBERGER

XEROX COLLEGE PUBLISHING
Lexington, Massachusetts / Toronto

PHOTOGRAPH CREDITS Jean Francois Petit: p. 124; Betty Binns: pp. 124, 126; Ken Heyman: p. 131

ACKNOWLEDGMENTS **Ambrose Bierce.** *Devil's Dictionary.* Dover, 1911; **George Bluestone.** *Novels into Film.* University of California Press, 1961, p. 1; **Jorge L. Borges.** "Borges and I" from his *Dreamtigers* translated by J. E. I. Reprinted by permission of the University of Texas Press; **Max Brandel.** "Dietician, from Hospital Signs We'd Like to See" from *The Fall to Mad Special,* Copyright © 1970 by E. C. Publications, Inc. Reprinted by permission of E. C. Publications, Inc.; **Augusto de Campos.** "Eye for Eye" from *An Anthology of Concrete Poetry* edited by Emmett Williams. Copyright © 1967 by Something Else Press, Inc. All rights reserved. Reproduced by permission of Something Else Press, Inc.; **Samuel Taylor Coleridge.** "Education of the Intellect by Awakening the Method of Self-Development."; **Father John Culkin.** *Film Study in the High School.* Fordham Film Study Center, 1965, pp. 21-22; **Leonardo Da Vinci.** "Mona Lisa." Courtesy of The Bettmann Archive, Inc.; **Sunny Decker.** *An Empty Spoon.* Harper and Row Publishers, Inc., 1970; **Charles Dickens.** "M'Choakumchild's Schoolroom." In Bernard Johnston, ed. *Issues in Education.* Houghton-Mifflin Company, 1964; **Dennis Dunn.** "Untitled." Copyright © 1969 by *Extensions.* Reprinted by permission of *Extensions*; **Frank Dunston.** Essay on Picasso's "Woman with Pears." Reprinted by permission of Frank Dunston; **Richard Eberhart.** "On a Squirrel Crossing the Road in New England" from his *Collected Poems 1930-1960.* Copyright © 1960 by Richard Eberhart. Reprinted by permission of Oxford University Press, Inc., and Chatto and Windus Ltd.; **Edward Fischer.** Excerpt from his *The Screen Arts.* Copyright © Sheed and Ward, Inc., 1960. Reprinted by permission of Sheed and Ward, Inc.; **Marsha Gardner.** "Time." Reprinted by permission of Marsha Gardner; **E. Gordon.** "Peace," 1968. Courtesy of Night Owl Posters; **D. W. Harding.** "Psychological Processes in the Reading of Fiction," *British Journal of Aesthetics,* II (1962), 140; **Vaclov Havel.** "Estrangement" from *An Anthology of Concrete Poetry* edited by Emmett Williams. Copyright © 1967 by Something Else Press, Inc. All rights reserved. Reproduced by permission of Something Else Press, Inc.; **Zbigniew Herbert.** "Armchairs" translated by Czeslaw Milosz from *Selected Poems* translated by Czeslaw Milosz and Peter Dale Scott. Translations copyright © 1968 by Czeslaw Milosz and Peter Dale Scott. Introduction copyright © 1968 by A. Alvarez. Reprinted by permission of Penguin Books, Ltd.; **Miroslav Holub.** "A Helping Hand" translated by George Theiner from *Selected Poems* translated by Ian Milner and George Theiner. Translations copyright © 1967 by Ian Milner and George Theiner. Introduction copyright © 1967 by A. Alvarez. Reprinted by permission of Penguin Books, Ltd.; **John Katz.** "An Integrated Approach to the Teaching of Film and Literature," *English Quarterly,* II, no. 1 (January 1969), 27; **Walt Kelly.** "Pogo." Copyright © 1970 by Walt Kelly. Courtesy of Publishers-Hall Syndicate; **Walt Kelly.** "Judge Parker." Courtesy of Publishers-Hall Syndicate; **Ruth Kraus.** "Play I (Pineapple Play)" from her *The Cantilever Rainbow.* Pantheon Books, a division of Random House, Inc. Copyright © 1963,

Designed by Betty Binns. Cover drawing by Charles A. Fredricks. Copyright © 1972 by Xerox Corporation. All rights reserved. No part of the material covered by this copyright may be produced in any form, or by any means of reproduction. Library of Congress Catalog Card Number: 71-185521. ISBN: 0-536-00694-6 Printed in the United States of America.

This book is dedicated
to those members of the
Modern Language Association
without whose work this
book would not have
had to be written

CONTENTS

PREFACE

Like so many others, this book grew out of a sense of lack. Unlike many others it grew out of a sense shared by people in many different parts of the country. The lack we sensed was one of both theory and practicality in the "new" teaching of literature in the schools. Seeing that teachers were struggling with exciting ideas about ways of dealing with literature, about using media or creative dramatics, about talking and writing in the classroom, and that through all this struggle there was a mingled sense of excitement and a sense of fear — seeing all this, we set about talking out and then writing down what we saw as ways of explaining why some of these new ways might be valuable, how they might be employed and integrated, and how they might lead to a cumulative program.

Our group divided up the responsibility for this book: Delores Minor is responsible for Chapter 3, Robert Weinberger for Chapter 4, Barbara Taylor for Chapter 5, Jerry L. Walker for Chapter 6, James Hoetker for Chapter 7, Wallace Douglas for Chapter 8, Sister Mary Owen S.N.D., and Robert Robinson for Chapter 10, and Alan Purves for Chapters 1, 2, 9 and the general editing.

We are grateful for the assistance of many: Phillip Thompson of the University of Wisconsin, Green Bay; Donald Rutledge of the Toronto Public Schools; Neil Kleinman; J. N. Hook; George Hendrick; and Bryant Fillion of the University of Illinois; Richard Nelson; Samuel Erskine and James Squire of Ginn and Company; Leslie Stratta and Carolyn Pierce of the Champaign Illinois Schools; Charles Suhor of the New Orleans Schools; and many other teachers, student teachers, and students at all levels. To Doris Hill who did the final typing we are ever in debt.

Our thanks, finally, to Nat LaMar and Betty Binns for the skillful and thoughtful and impossible job of bringing a conception into book form.

A.P.

**LIGHGHT
AND LIT 7**

A recent anthology of the best writing from American
literary magazines contained a poem called "Lighght" by Aram
Saroyan. The text of the poem is:

lighght

A popular television series "Lost in Space" ran a show one
week in which the plot hinged on a series of lines from T. S. Eliot.

Playboy and *Vogue* publish fiction that, ten years ago, would
have appeared in an esoteric literary quarterly. Of course *The
New Yorker* had been doing that long before; so had *Collier's*.

The Volkswagen ads with their "Think Small" brought to
advertising a sophistication quite different from the hucksterism
that marked most advertisers.

In a midwestern school a Black students' group was formed. One of the first activities was a writers' workshop and journal. One poem:

TIME

Life . . .
A child is born;
A plant grows;
Sand counts moments;
A clock ticks;
A second;
A minute;
—War!

— Time leaps on.

Death . . .
The child matures;
The plant withers;
The sand ceases;
The clock declines;
Post seconds;
Post hours;
Postwar —
Infinity.

— Time leaps on.

MARSHA GARDNER

Readers of *The Atom and Hawkman* comic books are expected
to be versed in molecular biology and Hindu mythology. Readers
of poetry are expected to grasp the allusions in this poem.

GOODBAT NIGHTMAN

God bless all policemen
and fighters of crime,
May thieves go to jail
for a very long time.

They've had a hard day
helping clean up the town,
Now they hang from the mantelpiece
both upside down.

A glass of warm blood
and then straight up the stairs,
Batman and Robin
are saying their prayers.

They've locked all the doors
and they've put out the bat,
Put on their batjamas
(They like doing that)

They've filled their batwater-bottles
made their batbeds,
With two springy battresses
for sleepy batheads.

They're closing red eyes
and they're counting black sheep,
Batman and Robin
are falling asleep.

ROGER MC GOUGH

KANSAS LAND

I would miss this Kansas land that I was leaving.
Wide prairie filled of green and cornstalk;
                              the flowering apple
Tall elms and oaks bordering streams that gurgle,
Rivers rolling quiet in long summers of sleepy days
For fishing, for swimming, for catching crawdad beneath the rock.
Cloud tufts billowing across the round blue sky.
Butterflies to chase through grass high as the chin.
Junebugs, swallowtails, red robin and bobolink,
Nights filled of soft laughter, fireflies and restless stars,
The winding sound of crickets rubbing dampness from their wings.
Silver September rain, orange-red-brown Octobers and white Decembers with hungry
Smells of hams and pork butts curing in the smokehouse.
Yes, all this I would miss — along with the fear, hatred and violence
We blacks had suffered upon this beautiful land.

GORDON PARKS

What's been happening to literature?

Not so long ago it seemed easy to stratify our cultural life into high-brow, middlebrow, and lowbrow; into mass-cult and mid-cult; or into popular and private. Whatever the name given to the stratum and no matter exactly how many strata were marked off, the notion of strata pervaded our thinking about our cultural life. There were those who like beer, baseball, and Batman; and those who liked Mahler, espresso, and Faulkner. Somewhere in the middle lay a group that listened to Hugo Winterhalter and belonged to the Book-of-the-Month-Club.

Into that stratified world, literature and literature-teaching fit very nicely. The task was simple. Given a group of students who, teachers were sure, preferred baseball and Batman to espresso and Faulkner, one simply had to present them with the best of "classical culture" from Sophocles to Joseph Conrad and trust that a larger percentage would end up subscribing to the Book-of-the-Month. One of the ways of presenting the material was to surround it with lots of biographical and historical information. Another way was to stretch the works out on a dissecting table, so as to analyze their patterns of imagery; search for ambiguities, puns, and paradoxes; and identify bits of synechdoche and metonymy. Still another way was to read what some scholar had written about one of the works and then set out to make the students come up with the scholar's interpretation. No matter the method; what was important was the students' "covering" the great works. At no point did the teacher question the *status quo*.

It was a nice plan — perhaps it did not fully accord with the way the world was, but it was a nice simple plan. To be sure, serious writers had long been working for the film companies, and poets were in advertising agencies, and some highbrows even liked baseball, but these must have been "aberrations."

Teachers did not mention the fact that William Faulkner had worked in Hollywood or H. L. Mencken had long attacked the pompous notions of what culture was, or that *The New Yorker* and *Esquire* had long sought to bring together the various facets of American culture.

For many teachers, what was happening in the world of book and magazine publishing or the world of films had nothing to do with literature classes. Then a number of things came along to upset their organized world. Television, mass enrollment in high schools and colleges, the surges in the circulation of the "mid-cult" magazines, and the incorporation of good writing and pornographic pictures within a single cover.

For good or bad, serious artists were taking popular culture seriously.

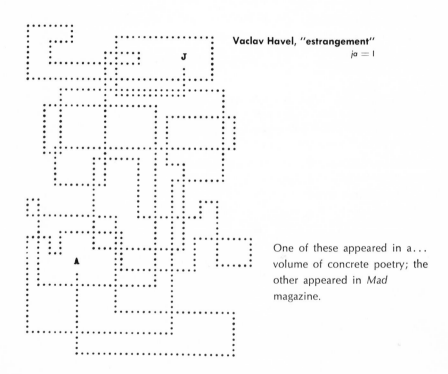

Vaclav Havel, "estrangement"

ja = I

One of these appeared in a... volume of concrete poetry; the other appeared in *Mad* magazine.

For good or bad, the understatements of the high culture became a part of the advertising world and thus a part of everybody's culture. For good or bad, writers became interested in how their books looked. For good or bad, photographers and cinematographers worked with writers, or, like photographer Gordon Parks, wrote themselves.

Another aspect of this change is the rise into deserved prominence of writers who had long been considered oddities. "Negro writer," "Jewish writer," "lady writer" were terms that helped people look down on Richard Wright, Irwin Shaw, or Willa Cather. Such terms cannot be used condescendingly today.

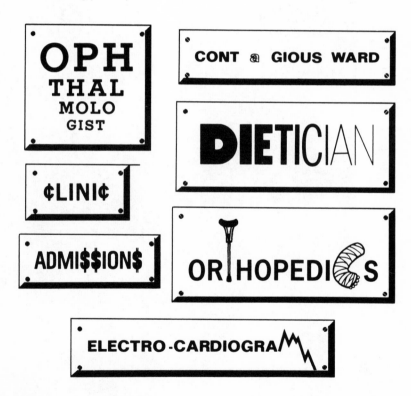

Twelve Rooftops Leaping

12 rooftops leaping
11 windows smashing
10 pipes abursting
9 sirens screaming
8 phone booths broken
7 bulbs adimming
6 junkies trading
5 stolen rings
4 padlocked stores
3 slashed tires
2 cherry bombs

And a scout group planting a tree.

Everything got mixed up even
more than it had been

We now have such a cross fertilization between "high" and "low" culture in our writing that to use such a distinction to put down a writer doesn't make much sense (good and bad, yes; but high and low, no).

We now have a mingling of writing and the graphic arts (and the aural arts) into a mélange of media. Literature refuses to rest securely in 10-point type on the page. Literature includes both scripted and improvised theater, film, television drama, and happenings.

Much of it demands to be looked at, to be heard, to be read all at once. It demands to be taken as fun. Fun that had its serious moments, but fun nevertheless. Eve Merriam can place a poem of social protest in the setting of a Christmas carol.

It demands that we enjoy it and feel its power.

It demands that we respond to it creatively.

A HELPING HAND

We gave a helping hand to grass —
  and it turned into corn.
We gave a helping hand to fire —
  and it turned into a rocket.
Hesitatingly,
cautiously,
we give a helping hand
to people,
to some people . . .

MIROSLAV HOLUB

Narrator
In a poem you make your point with pineapples.

(PINEAPPLES fly onto stage from all directions.)

Spy
And it would be nice to have a spy going in and out.

End

RUTH KRAUSS

Literature demands to be taken naturally.

Most of all I like writing for people untouched by poetry for instance, for those who do not even know that it should be at all for them. I would like them to read poems as naturally as they read the papers, or go to a football game. Not to consider it as anything more difficult, or effeminate, or praiseworthy
writes the Czech biologist-poet Miroslav Holub.

Kenneth Koch has shown that children in the primary grades can write good poems by any standard.

Literature demands even more strongly than ever before that the traditional barriers between genres be looked at as inconsequential, that such classification fails because it does not provide useful distinctions.

BORGES AND I

The other one, the one called Borges, is the one things happen to. I walk through the streets of Buenos Aires and stop for a moment, perhaps mechanically now, to look at the arch of an entrance hall and the grillwork on the gate; I know of Borges from the mail and see his name on a list of professors or in a biographical dictionary. I like hourglasses, maps, eighteenth-century typography, the taste of coffee and the prose of Stevenson; he shares these preferences, but in a vain way that turns them into the attributes of an actor. It would be an exaggeration to say that ours is a hostile relationship; I live, let myself go on living, so that Borges may contrive his literature, and this literature justifies me. It is no effort for me to confess that he has achieved some valid pages, but those pages cannot save me, perhaps because what is good belongs to no one, not even to him, but rather to the language and to tradition. Besides, I am destined to perish, definitively, and only some instant of myself can survive in him. Little by little, I am giving over everything to him, though I am quite aware of his perverse custom of falsifying and magnifying things. Spinoza knew that all things long to persist in their being; the stone eternally wants to be a stone and the tiger a tiger. I shall remain in Borges, not in myself (if it is true that I am someone), but I recognize myself less in his books than in many others or in the laborious strumming of a guitar. Years ago I tried to free myself from him and went from the mythologies of the suburbs to the games with time and infinity, but those gmaes belong to Borges now and I shall have to imagine other things. Thus my life is a flight and I lose everything and everything belongs to oblivion, or to him.

I do not know which of us has written this page.

TRANSLATED BY J. E. I.

concrete poetry

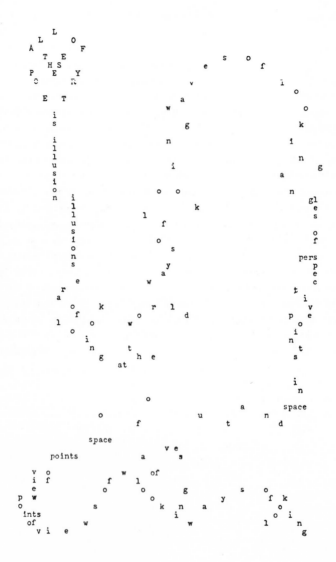

Yet literature, like all art demands to be taken seriously: When you make a poem you merely speak or write the language of every day, capturing as many bonuses as possible and economizing on losses; that is, you come awake to what always goes on in language, and you use it to the limit of your ability and your power of attention at the moment. You always fail, to some extent, since the opportunities are infinite — but think of the extent of your failure in ordinary conversation! Poetry bears the brunt, though; for in trying for the best it calls attention to its vivid failures.
WILLIAM STAFFORD

It even demands that the traditional language barriers be broken. Good translations of poets abound. Fiction and drama have become virtually international: witness the awarding of a National Book Award to a Brazilian novel; witness thirty companies of *Hair*; witness the polyglot or monoglot (depending on how you look at it) cinema.

It has long demanded not to be censored and has taken everything for its province: Hamlet, homosexuality, sadism, smog, masturbation, the flag, black Masses, computers, and race. Revolution has been the topic of poems printed in the more staid journals.

"Literature," once the private preserve of the cultivated happy few, has become anarchic, joyful, and vital.

In fact, the term *literature* hardly applies to this congeries of writing, graphics, sound, music, film, and tape.

Forms are breaking down; the regularity of print is challenged; taboos of subject matter are breaking down; but mere anarchy is not loosed upon the world. Literature is undergoing one of its perennial shifts whereby every convention is being tested and used as the springboard for trying out new modes of expression.

Where have the old values gone?

It depends on what values you mean. If it is the value of the able expression of a meaningful experience, that value has remained. If it is the "value" of a classic being a classic just because someone thought it was a classic and everyone had to worship it as a classic, that value has come under increasing attack.

Value has remained, but values and evaluators and the literary stock market have come under increasing attack. The criteria by which people judge pieces of writing have been challenged. Who says a work must end with a period, must have a single static form, must accord to the "rules" of a genre, must deal with the niceties, must be written by one person, or even by a person? Who says great literature must always be about man's deepest thoughts or must be taken seriously? Who says that a work must have a single meaning? Who says a work must use words?

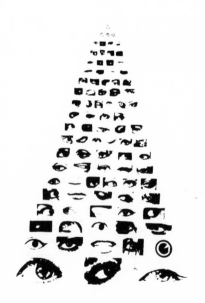

All of these matters are matters of taste, and taste is subject to change.

Values have remained, but they are continually tested and challenged by new creations. One value that has remained is the value of pleasure. Literature seeks to please the person who made it and the person who attends to it. Pleasure is not the same as laughter, but is a sense that what is written is as it should be.

Has this bursting the bonds of convention, genre, standards never happened before?

Of course it has. It happened when the Elizabethans played hob with dramatic form and with the Italian sonnet. It happened when opera introduced the mixing of media. It happened with the novel in the eighteenth century. It happened with poetry in almost every generation. Writers have continually sought to "make it new," to modify the conventions set by their predecessors and to forge their own forms, themes, combinations of words, of media, of ideas. Often they have failed; often they have succeeded.

Today's writers are no different, save that they have more traditions to play against, more gadgets to play with, more areas of information to assimilate into their writing, and — most important of all — a larger literate audience.

What makes the plethora of writings, forms, themes, mixtures, seem inchoate to many English teachers is that literary education has gotten itself all mixed up with writers and what they do. A couple of hundred years ago, the schools taught Latin and Greek. English and American literature were not part of the school or college curriculum (save for a few excerpts that were used to teach people how to read). Writers wrote.

When education became the province of all, Latin and Greek literature were replaced by English literature, but it was the English literature of the sixteenth, seventeenth, and eighteenth centuries. In the universities this literature was studied historically, connected with the development of the language and with the moral and political life of the times in which it was written. In the high schools, works were read for their beauty of expression and their purity of thought — read, that is, as models of ethics and style. Writers went on writing.

Magpielike Chaucer borrowed plots, themes, lines from contemporary writers as well as from the "classics." He also had fun poking holes in literary conventions.

So did Shakespeare:

My mistress' eyes are nothing like the sun;
Coral is far more red than her lips' red:
If snow be white, why then her breasts are dun;
If hairs be wires, black wires grow in her head.
I have seen roses damasked, red and white,
But no such roses see I in her cheeks;
And in some perfumes is there more delight
Than in the breath that from my mistress reeks.
I love to hear her speak, yet well I know
That music hath a far more pleasing sound:
I grant I never saw a goddess go, —
My mistress, when she walks, treads on the ground:
    And yet, by heaven, I think my love as rare
    As any she belied with false compare.

Sonnet 130

Thomas Carlyle was so unsatisfied with the form of the philosophical thesis that he invented a German writer and an editor to present his ideas. The result was *Sartor Resartus*.

When *Moby Dick* came out, the critics all condemned it for not fitting any of their literary categories.

Ambrose Bierce found that one of the most congenial forms for him was the "Dictionary." In his *Devil's Dictionary*, he defines a critic:

CRITIC, n. A person who boasts himself hard to please because nobody tries to please him.

There is a land of pure delight,
Beyond the Jordan's flood,
Where saints, apparelled all in white,
Fling back the critic's mud.

And as he legs it through the skies,
His pelt a sable hue,
His sorrows sore to recognize
The missles that he threw.

Orrin Gool

During the course of this century, the university study of literature has attained the proportions of a big business. Pieces of writing have acquired barnacles of articles, books, and dissertations, with definitive editions, annotated editions, scholarly editions, variorum editions; with examinations of structure, imagery, and metaphor; with interpretations political, social, psychological, aesthetic, and moral; with computerized concordances and bibliographies of bibliographies. Shakespeare, needless to say, has become the most encrusted. Students who want to know all that has been said about *Hamlet* would have to spend their lifetimes reading.

In the schools, this industry has shown itself in the many curriculum guides and teaching aides that accompany each text, in the revolving book-racks of drugstores, which are often filled not with novels, poems, plays, and nonfiction, but with master outlines and study guides to the great works. The accumulation of knowledge and secondhand opinions about what writers have written has superseded the reading and enjoying of what they have written. Literary study, even in the junior high school, is a very serious business, wherein meanings, structures, ambiguities, and backgrounds take the place of reading, responding, and enjoying. All of

this study requires that literature be seen as a fixed entity, that the text exist as data, that the definitions of *poem, irony, point-of-view, metaphor* be fixed so that it can be taught to children the way multiplication tables and the parts of speech are taught to children.

And writers go on writing.

Writers don't seem to pay too much attention to what goes on in school. Have they forgotten what they have been taught? Or is it that they, like so many of their predecessors, have realized that literature methodized becomes a literature that stagnates?

Don't be fooled into thinking that literary scholarship is valueless. On the contrary, critical commentary, historical study, textual editing, bibliographical enterprise all are valuable, particularly to teachers, not because they give us the truth that they purport to give us, but because they allow us to see the ways in which people have responded to pieces of writing. They have become a testimony to the power of the mind to read, and to construct and test hypotheses about what it reads. They form a testimony to the ability of man to organize and build structures out of a collocation of objects that might be considered unique were it not for man's structure-building capacities.

Like the scientists' elaborate organization of natural phenomena, like the historians' network connecting human events and actions, like the psychologists' theories of human behavior, the literary scholars' web of biographical, historical, generic, structural, archetypal, and rhetorical connections between poem and poem, between play and play, between novel and essay is a triumph. But it is not the same thing as works it deals with, just as science is not nature and history is not human events.

Sing, goddess, the anger of Peleus' son Achilleus
and its devastation, which put pains thousandfold upon the Achaians,
hurled in their multitudes to the house of Hades strong souls. . . .
of heroes, but gave their bodies to be the delicate feasting
of dogs. . . .

What happens to a dream deferred?

The curfew tolls the knell of parting day,
The lowing herd wind slowly o'er the lea,
The plowman homeward plods his weary way,
And leaves the world to darkness and to me.

When shall we three meet again?
In thunder, lightning, or in rain. . . .

I am an invisible man.

They told me Heraclitus, they told me you were dead. . . .

It is a truth universally acknowledged, that a single man in possession
of a good fortune must be in want of a wife.

Let us go then, you and I,
While the evening is spread out against the sky. . . .

"You, Tom!"

By and by
Call me Ishmael.   God caught his eye. . . .

I'm lighting out for the territory.

That time of year thou mayst in me behold. . . .

ARMCHAIRS

Who ever thought a warm neck would become an armrest, or
legs eager for flight and joy could stiffen into four simple
stilts? Armchairs were once noble flower-rating creatures.
However, they allowed themselves too easily to be domesticated
and today they are the most wretched species of quadrupeds.
They have lost all their stubbornness and courage. They are
only meek. They haven't trampled anyone or galloped off with
anyone. They are, for certain, conscious of a wasted life.
     The despair of armchairs is revealed in their creaking.

ZBIGNIEW HERBERT

Literature is ... but *literature* isn't; there is perhaps no such thing as *literature*. As far as general education is concerned there are poems, and plays, and stories, and cartoons, and jokes, but *literature*? *Literature* is an abstraction, a network. For different people, *literature* is different networks. For some it is all the information about authors and publishers and audiences; just the way for some the Beatles were everything about Paul, Ringo, George, and John but their music. For some it is an elaborate code set forth to trap the unwary reader who must continually read between the lines. For some it is an infinite series of changes upon a few themes. For some it is a verbal manifestation of the totality of man's psyche — a model of man.

Perhaps the broadest definition is one that states: It is a vast assortment of verbal (usually) utterances, each of which comes from some writer, who has a voice; and each of which in itself has some order. It includes *Mary Worth* and the *Divine Comedy*. Pieces of literature are such as to arouse a response — a sense of knowing, a sense of feeling, a sense of moving — in me. When these senses coalesce I have a kind of pleasure, a sense of the fitness of things. Out of having read what I've read, I construct a theory — a theory building upon the nature of language and upon the nature of the mind and upon the meeting of language and mind in what I would call response.

But if what you have said is true, then your definition of literature doesn't matter? does it?

Of course not.

COLUMN A		COLUMN B
sounds		feelings
syllables		memories
type faces		concepts
words		stereotypes
phrases		word associations
images		sound associations
metaphors	**Take**	word meanings
logical relationships	**each from**	favorite rhythms
characters	**Column A**	syntactic expectations
actions	**and each**	ideas about people
symbols	**from**	ideas about society
settings	**Column B**	ideas about nature
paragraphs	**Connect**	ideas about abstractions
meters	**each to**	previous works read
rhythms	**every other**	political beliefs
figures of speech	**and enjoy**	religious beliefs
dialogue	**your literary**	criteria about form
description	**theory**	subconscious desires
narration		moral censor
action		ego drive
pictures		psychological state
tones		aesthetic criteria
perspectives		sense of what is significant
moods		theory of literature
poems		philosophy of life. . . .
plays		
stories		
epics. . . .		

Well, then, what about literature courses?

At the center of the curriculum are *not* the works of literature, those collections of words in print or in sound wave, or the individual psyche with its neurological movements and its constantly changing psychological states and constantly modifying sets of images and concepts . . .

but

all those lines connecting the two. The mind as it meets the book. The response. That is the center of a curriculum in literature. Treat those lines carefully, or the book will become dead and the mind will retreat into itself. But treat those lines and you will have a response-centered curriculum.

THE
RESPONSE-CENTERED
CURRICULUM

FOUR OBJECTIVES OF A RESPONSE-CENTERED PROGRAM

a *An individual will feel secure in his response to a poem and not be dependent on someone else's response. An individual will trust himself.*

b *An individual will know why he responds the way he does to a poem — what in him causes that response and what in the poem causes that response. He will get to know himself.*

c *An individual will respect the responses of others as being as valid for them as his is for him. He will recognize his differences from other people.*

d *An individual will recognize that there are common elements in people's responses. He will recognize his similarity with other people.*

The basic process connecting the onlooker with any event, real or fictional, involving living things, is that of imagining. The fundamental fact is that we can imagine ourselves in a situation very different from the one we are in, we can create images of the sensations we should have, we can become aware, in part, of the meanings we should see in it, what our intentions, attitudes, and emotions would be, what satisfactions and frustrations we should experience.

D. W. HARDING

"Response-centered program" is a pretentious but fairly accurate definition the way we suggest literature should be taught in the 1970s.

Of course you don't teach literature, or English, you teach students or children. We all know that. People, not things, are the focus of instruction. Recently too much attention has been paid to things, and people have been forgotten.

Of course, people learn all by themselves. People have done it for years. They have learned lots of things without teachers, and outside classrooms. One of the best ways people have devised for learning is by doing things and then by figuring out what they have done and why they have done it. If they like what they have done, they try to repeat the operation.

Doing things and looking at yourself while and after you have done them is what this program is about.

That's why this is a response-centered program. It is not focused only on the child. Nor is it focused entirely on the literary works and literature. It's not subject centered or child centered. It deals with what happens when child meets subject. That way, it's child-and-subject centered.

But we like to call it response centered. Because responding, responding creatively, is what people do.

Poet: Thomas Hood
19th Century
Epigram

SATIRE

What is a modern Poet's fate?
To write his thoughts upon a slate;
The critic spits on what is done,
Gives it a wipe — and all is gone!

ENGLAND -

WORLD Associations

Family

Teachers

Other Poems

schools

MEMORY

There's a poem, written by somebody, and that somebody has a life and a history and an environment.

There's a reader who is somebody with his world of images, metaphors, symbols; and that somebody has a life and a history and an environment.

The reader reads the poem and something happens:

he understands what the words say to him

he translates the experience he has read about into his own context

he has a feeling about the experience

he has attitudes about the experience and the poem.

He takes the words, and the images, and the experiences and ideas of that poem; and he puts them into his own way of seeing things. He reads a poem with the word *snapped.* Maybe he sees a gingersnap, maybe he sees someone snapping his fingers, maybe it makes him feel funny or sad, maybe he doesn't understand that the word could mean *to talk sharply.*

On the basis of that process, the reader might

draw a picture

groan

talk about the poem

improvise a little skit

laugh

write a paragraph

make a film

try to forget he read the silly thing.

That's his response: part of it's inside him, part of it's expressed. We all do it. We've been doing it for years. Even critics do it. Saying we respond to pieces of literature is like saying we have been talking prose all our lives.

**The particular response depends on
what is being responded to**

THEODORE HELPGOD
Stranger! I died of hydrophobia.
I was bitten by both the upper and the under dog.
While trying to save the under dog.

E. L. MASTERS

THE SUDDEN CHILLNESS
The piercing chill I feel:
   my dead wife's comb, in our bedroom,
   under my heel . . .

TANIGUCHI BUSON
(1715–83)

Those two are quite different.

The pieces differ
sounds   *words*   *characters*   *images*   *locales*   *incidents*

The ways of gluing the pieces together differ
arrangement   *syntax*   *plot*   *structure*   *pattern*   *tone*
mood   *voice*   *total shape.*

You could even take the same pieces and glue them differently and get
a different work.

Stranger, While trying to save the underdog,
I was bitten by both the upper and the under dog.
I died of hydrophobia.

**The particular response we make
depends on who is responding**

People differ in their experience. Many have never been to the seashore. Many have read lots of comic books. Many have been in wars. Some have lost a father or a mother. Their past experience affects their response.

People differ in their concepts of things. Say "America" to a group of ten people and ask them to say what their concept of it is. You probably will get ten different concepts.

People differ in their attitudes toward things. Not everybody hates school or *Silas Marner* or the Doors.

People differ in their interests. Not everybody watches the 6:00 news on the same channel. Some even turn off the set.

All of these and many other differences affect even the way people perceive things. If you love a boy, you see him in a crowd. You don't "see" the other people. If you read a letter, or a list, you see your name, not all the other names.

If these differences affect the way people see things, they also affect the kinds of reactions they have to things, and the kinds of actions they perform in response to things.

Look again at the poem on page 24 of this book; jot down all the things that come to mind. Get a friend to do the same thing. Are the jottings more alike or more different?

Then do it again next week. Have your jottings changed?

. . . it would look as though texts themselves are in great jeopardy. They are. The moment we subject them to real rather than theoretical readers, they enter the actual world of human confrontations in which everything is in jeopardy. At the same time nothing I have said argues against the reader's obligation to try with all his resources to understand and feel the point of view, vision, and meanings of the work itself. Nor need such a pursuit be urged on the grounds of objectivity alone, for any morality which requires respect for the uniqueness and otherness of things outside the self requires that same respect be extended to works of art. What I am saying is that real respect requires not a suspension or withholding of the self and its full awarenesses but an exercise and offering of them.

WALTER SLATOFF

In a reading that results in a work of art, the reader is concerned with the quality of the experience that he is living through under the stimulus and guidance of the text. No one else can read the poem or the novel or the play for him. To ask someone else to experience a work of art for him would be tantamount to seeking nourishment by asking someone else to eat his dinner for him.

LOUISE ROSENBLATT

If people are different and if stories and poems and plays are different, then we can say that different people respond differently to different pieces of writing (or painting, or whatever). There are only unique responses.

**IF ALL RESPONSES ARE UNIQUE, THEN
THERE IS NOTHING FOR THE TEACHER TO DO,
RIGHT??**

                                            wrong

There is a great deal for the teacher to do

*The teacher must provide each student with as many different works
as possible.*

*The teacher must encourage each student to respond as fully as he
is able.*

*The teacher must encourage the student to understand why he responds
as he does.*

*The teacher must encourage the student to respond to as many works
as possible.*

*The teacher must encourage the student to tolerate responses that
differ from his.*

*The teacher must encourage students to explore their areas of
agreement and disagreement.*

Although works are unique and people are unique and responses are
unique, there are points where responses touch and overlap. The following
are three points of agreement:

If everybody in a group is responding to the same poem, the common
point is the poem.

If a person is responding to a poem, a play, and a novel, the common
point is the person.

If a group of people are talking about novels they have read, the common point is the language they are using to talk with.

THE SEA

Poor boy. He had very big ears, and when he would turn his back to the window they would become scarlet. Poor boy. He was bent over, yellow. The man who cured came by behind his glasses. "The sea," he said, "the sea, the sea." Everyone began to pack suitcases and speak of the sea. They were in a great hurry.

The boy figured that the sea was like being inside a tremendous seashell full of echoes and chants and voices that would call from afar with a long echo. He thought that the sea was tall and green, but when he arrived at the sea, he stood still. His skin, how strange it was there. "Mother," he said because he felt ashamed, "I want to see how high the sea will come on me." He who thought that the sea was tall and green, saw it white like the head of a beer — tickling him, cold on the tips of his toes.

"I am going to see how far the sea will come on me." And he walked, he walked, he walked and the sea, what a strange thing! — grew and became blue, violet. It came up to his knees. Then to his waist, to his chest, to his lips, to his eyes. Then into his ears there came a long echo and the voices that call from afar. And in his eyes all the color. Ah, yes, at last the sea was true. It was one great, immense seashell. The sea truly was tall and green.

But those on the shore didn't understand anything about anything. Above they began to cry and scream and were saying "What a pity, Lord, what a great pity."

ANNA MARIA MATUTE
Spanish

To take the first common point first: A story like the one on the opposite page has a set number of words and a set order of words.

Those words have a limited, although not strictly limited, range of meanings. "Poor" can mean *unfortunate* in not being rich, in not being healthy, in not being happy, in not being lucky, and so forth. . . .

Odds are that it does not mean *happy*.

"The man who cured came by behind his glasses" can hardly be reconstructed as "The glasses who cured came by behind the man" unless you wanted to change what had been written.

A story like the one on the opposite page has a set order of incidents. The boy goes to the sea after he is at home, not before.

The story also contains only the incidents and people it contains. For the purposes of this story, the boy might as well have no grandfather and no sister. He might or might not have been locked in his room for three weeks prior to the opening of the story. It has a set number of people speaking: a narrator, a boy, a man, some other people. At times it is hard to tell whether the boy or the narrator is speaking, but at those times, the choice is limited to those two.

These are some of the limits set by the text.

Here are some limits NOT set by the text:

Whether the boy is sick with tuberculosis
Whether the boy is young or old
Whether the boy wants to die
Whether the man who cured is a doctor or a minister
Whether the narrator likes the boy or not
Whether the narrator approves of the boy
Whether the boy knows that he is going to die
Whether the parents love the boy
Whether he loves his parents
Whether the colors have any significance
Whether the boy is imaginative
Whether the people on the shore are unimaginative
Whether the narrator agrees with the people on the shore
Whether those on the shore are spiritually dead
Whether those on the shore represent some abstract force or idea
Whether the author admires the boy for what he did
Whether the author agrees with the narrator
Whether the author thinks those on the shore are ignorant
Whether the story is triumphant, sad, or ironic, or all three
Whether there is a lesson to be learned from the story
Whether the story is well constructed
Whether the story is moving
Whether the story is meaningful to the twentieth-century reader
Whether the story is a classic
Whether the author subscribes to a philosophical position
Whether the whole story takes place in the boy's mind
Whether the author is a great writer
Whether the author is a woman
Whether the author and the story are . . .

To take the second common point: Some of the ways by which an individual's responses to several works may have something in common include the words and word structures he knows; the experiences he has had; the prejudices he has acquired; his ability to tell about the connotation and implication of certain words; whether he can visualize images, or whether his imagination is more auditory or kinetic; his openness to new experiences; the preconceptions he has formed.

To take the third common point: Most people have some things in common.

most people have roughly the same meaning of some words in their heads;

most people have comparable experiences of some things;

most people have similar judgments of human behavior; they know whom to trust, what motivates people to do what they do;

most people have comparable emotional reactions to such things as colors, sound patterns, actions of certain people;

most people make similar judgments about some things, like what they saw if they were watching a television show — they saw a person riding a horse, not a series of light and dark dots.

Most people can agree that it is possible for different people to make different judgments about some things — whether it was a good guy or a bad guy riding that horse — and nobody being absolutely sure.

So . . .

the text limits our response

the limits of human nature limit our response

our ability to communicate limits our response

STILL SCIENTIFIC RESEARCH SHOWS THAT
THERE ARE A MINIMUM OF 500,000,000,000
POSSIBLE DIFFERENT RESPONSES TO A GIVEN TEXT.
THAT'S AT LEAST 200 DIFFERENT RESPONSES
FOR EVERYBODY IN THE WORLD!

And they are all related.

Given the diversity and connectedness of people's responses to what they read or see, the educational goal becomes one of helping the student recognize both that diversity and that connectedness.

Enter:

THE RESPONSE-CENTERED CURRICULUM

It recognizes people's diversity, and it encourages that diversity.

It recognizes the connections between people and encourages people to make them manifest in sharing their responses with a group.

It recognizes that response is joyous.

Its procedure is simple:

The teacher encourages each person to express whatever his response might be, and encourages everyone to exchange responses or share in expressing a response freely. As people work together, they modify their individuality where it seems appropriate, retain it where it seems appropriate. As people work together, they find out about other people and about themselves. The teacher's role is to challenge people to justify, explain, and share their responses.

Its aim is to have people come to a greater knowledge of why they are who they are, and thus approach new works of literature with greater self-confidence.

Its aim is to affect people's perception of works of art (literary works), to affect their ability to articulate their responses, and to affect their tolerance of the diversity of human responses to similar objects.

A girl gushes over a story that the class has just read, and she says it is just lovely, she could just see everything as if it were there, and it was so moving. Another girl replies, "That's baloney." Silence. *The teacher asks why she said that.* Without defending or attacking either one, the teacher asks both to be more explicit.

A boy reads "The Sea" and decides to make a film. "I want to film that down at the park." "So do I," say four others. *The teacher asks them how they would film it.* Better yet, the teacher gets a camera or encourages the student to get one and lets them go off and film it. Then the group can compare the film and the story and their responses to each.

Suppose a boy sits stolidly, blankly as others talk about a play. *Later the teacher asks him why he was silent.* Didn't he like it? "Yeah, but I don't want to talk about it." Be quiet . . . that time. Later, perhaps the next day, the teacher asks him why he didn't want to talk yesterday. There is no embarrassment.

Suppose a girl sits quietly for a few minutes while the rest talk animatedly about a story they have read. The teacher asks why. "I don't know what you want me to say," she bursts out. *The teacher replies, "It's not what I want you to say that matters; it's my job to help you say what you want to say."*

Suppose the teacher asks people to jot down their thoughts about a story. "But it didn't involve me or interest me." "This story has no point to it." "The title is very significant." "It reads like it was written for a fourth-grader." "It was boring." "The action adds flavor to the story and makes a good end." *The teacher cites these points to the class and has them talk out their differences.* Can they convince each other? How? Why or why not? What is each of them saying?

Just how does this program proceed?

very carefully (like those porcupines)

The teacher assumes little about the children save that they can attend to pieces of writing by listening or reading, and that when they read or hear a piece of writing they will respond in many ways. The teacher then presents something — like a story — to the children

. . . and waits

. . . and watches

. . . and listens

The children may decide to remain silent; they may get up and decide to act something out; they may decide to draw, to make a film, a collage, a song medley; they may decide to hear the story again or turn to something else in the book; or they may decide to talk. And not all of them will decide to do the same thing at the same time.

The teacher must allow the children this first opportunity to express their responses. It may take a long time or a short time. It may seem dull to the teacher or seem nonintellectual or stupid or philistine. It may be exciting for the children; it's new for them, so accept what they do as genuine, listen, watch, attend to what they are doing and take notes — mental or written. Help those who want to express something, express what they want to express. At the moment when you think the children have expressed their initial responses fully, ask them to clarify, to expand, to explain, to share more fully. Encourage them to ask this of each other — not to put each other down but to understand what each is doing, and why.

Suppose that after having read Pope's *An Essay on Man* some students decide to make a collage about the aspects of modern man — a collage Essay on Man. *After they have finished the teacher asks them whether they think they have captured the movement of the poem as well as its statement.*

Suppose a group of students start complaining about the anthology they are using. *The teacher asks them to make up their own.* As they begin, the teacher asks them what decisions they have to make, decisions about size, type of selection, whether to have only contemporary selections, what sorts of illustrations and graphic treatment there will be.

Suppose a group of students decide that a poem has a really interesting beat. *The teacher asks them to demonstrate this beat, offers the use of a tape recorder in helping them record what they mean.*

Suppose a student complains that he can't read the story . . . so he doesn't get what the class is talking about. *If it seems appropriate, after class in a conference, the teacher reads the story aloud to the student.* If they are in class, the teacher suggests that some of the others dramatize the story; then all have something to respond to.

Suppose a group of students wonder what would happen if they had read a poem and had not known what its title was; would they have responded differently? *The teacher asks if they want to try an experiment with another class and sets up a research project that the group can carry out.*

The teacher selects some of the material.

The students select some too.

The teacher suggests alternate forms of response.

If the students are talking, the teacher might suggest that they write.

The teacher structures particular forms of expressing response.

At some points it is interesting and fun for everyone to improvise the end of a story. Even if they themselves haven't finished it, they can imagine what might happen.

The teacher structures particular modes of response.

At some points it is interesting and fun to ask the group, "But what do YOU *think it* MEANS?"

The teacher works to elicit the fullest possible response.

At some points the teacher must be dogged about asking, "Why?" "What do you mean?" "Tell us more." "I don't understand."

The teacher calls the students' attention to certain parts of the work.

At times the teacher may ask how a comparison, a word, a character affects what a student said. Does it change his response?

The teacher encourages the students to be their own teachers, to teach each other.

At times the students must suggest alternate forms of response to each other, must suggest other material,

The teacher encourages the students to teach the teacher.

must determine modes of response, must ask each other to elaborate or check responses,

The teacher encourages the students to try new things.

to point out parts of the work that might lead to different responses.

Most of all, the teacher seeks to make the students aware of how much they already know, how much they already feel, how much they already understand. The teacher encourages the students to be articulate, creative.

What about all the information that people have to have to really know a poem or a story?

In a sense, all the information people really have to have is in the words and structure of words of the text. There are useful terms — *story, poem, word, repetition, scene, pattern, narrator* or *speaker, comparison.* There are a few terms — *metaphor, symbol, plot, irony, rhyme, rhythm, voice, point of view, allegory* — that are also useful, but not absolutely necessary. And there are a lot of terms — *metonymy, anacrusis, iamb, sonnet, heroic couplet, bildungsroman, litotes,* and *romantic irony* — that belong to the specialist and become a part of his jargon but are quite unnecessary for most people.

The situation is just like that in any field: the same thing can be a *pitch* or a *reverse knuckle ball*: the same thing can be a *leap* or a *jetée*; the same thing can be a layer cake or a kaiser's torte. One term is more precise than the other, but either is sufficient for most communication, particularly when the people talking about the thing are trying to understand each other as well as the thing.

The critical language that developed came from man's need to classify and categorize his experiences. It came from the same impetus that has led to the elaborate classifications of plant and animal life. In a sense, of course, education is the learning of these classificatory schemes, but too often the learning of the names of plants has replaced looking at them, smelling them, enjoying them. The same thing has happened to reading.

In a response-centered curriculum, the central focus is the experience of the reader with the text. In order to insure that this focus remains central, the learning of classificatory terms and critical descriptors needs to be held to a minimum. Too easily can it become the center of attention.

In order to make any sensible critical statement, a person needs only the resources of a nonspecialist's lexicon.

Does it affect your understanding of "The Pit and the Pendulum" to know that Poe drank?

Does it affect your judgment of "Jabberwocky" to know that Lewis Carroll's real name was Dodgson?

Does it affect your interest in Tom and Becky in the cave to know that Mark Twain was a staunch atheist?

In fact, does it affect your understanding, appreciation, interpretation, judgment, or involvement to know whether The Tempest *should properly be called a romance or a tragicomedy?*

Of course it does, and of course it does not. But there is a time for all that information, and that is the time when people are in training to be literary critics, literary historians, literature teachers, or quiz-show question writers. It is not the time when people are learning how best to express what has happened when they met with "The Pit and the Pendulum," "Jabberwocky," *Tom Sawyer,* or *The Tempest.*

Then there's all that information about the author and his life, the history of the work, or the fact that drama started as religious ritual, or the specific references to English politics in *Gulliver's Travels.* Yes, that affects a person's response; it may even give him a different kind of response than the one he would have if he were reading the work without any such information. Is his response the better for having all this information? No. No worse. The two responses are different.

One of the problems with the teaching of literature is that all this sort of information seems to crowd the response of the reader to the text out of the center of the stage. The students get everything but the work. In some countries, literature classes consist of almost nothing except reading literary histories. The students don't read the things the histories are about. In part, this happens because it's much easier to make up a test of factual knowledge than it is to evaluate a response-centered curriculum — or even an analytic curriculum.

Be that as it may, background information should be precisely what it is called "background." At times it should be so far back it is out of sight.

Adolescents will probably not enjoy much of the fiction about the end of marriage; Joyce's "The Dead" is not a good selection to assign to sixteen-year-olds.

It would probably be better to present Shakespeare's Troilus and Cressida *than* King Lear *in a twelfth-grade class.*

Adolescents will probably get more out of Franz Kafka's allegories than they will out of Thomas Mann's philosophical novels.

Billy Budd *will probably be more successful than* Moby Dick *with a group of eleventh-graders.*

Shelley's political poems will probably evoke a more energetic response than will his poems about art like "To a Skylark."

E. E. Cummings's exuberant language will probably gain more adherents to poetry than T. S. Eliot's measured language.

Better to elicit responses with James Thurber than with Charles Lamb.

Take Tarzan on man and nature rather than John Stuart Mill or Alfred, Lord Tennyson.

Use modern Black writers rather than Harriet Beecher Stowe.

Mad *magazine is as effective an exponent of satire as Addison or Steele.*

BEST YET
try all of these
and do not be bound to any
preconception.

All right, but isn't it important for a student to have read the classics?

useful, yes,

important?

Many of the "classics" are not classics. Often, the second-rate work of a major writer is used in the schools, because the first-rate is "too old for him." Children have suffered through *Silas Marner* for years and learned to hate George Eliot for her poorer book and therefore never read the better one, *Middlemarch*.

Often the work is "too old" for a great number of students. It might deal with a series of emotions and thoughts that adolescents find hard to cope with — such is the case with most of what Wordsworth wrote, and most of what Milton wrote, too. Rather than water it down, or choose poor selections by the same author, or force it down students' throats, a teacher might just forget about it for now. Of course it is hard to tell what is too old. It depends so much on the individual.

Often the inclusion of the classics causes a bad reaction. Teachers tend to want to worship a classic and force students to worship it, too. Students tend to see classics as "irrelevant" because they are not able to see that there is a great degree of generalizability from the classic to their lives. Is *Billy Budd* irrelevant because it's about sailing ships? It's also about the problem of relating ends to means, the problem of making unpleasant decisions. Those problems are relevant to the students' world — but it is often hard to see that, when you are so wrapped up in the world.

I shall take as my clue for this investigation the well-known fact that the aim of a skilful performance is achieved by the observance of a set of rules which are not known as such to the person following them. For example, the decisive factor by which the swimmer keeps himself afloat is the manner by which he regulates his respiration; he keeps his buoyancy at an increased level by refraining from emptying his lungs when breathing out and by inflating them more than usual when breathing in: yet this is not generally known to swimmers. A well-known scientist, who in his youth had to support himself by giving swimming lessons, told me how puzzled he was when he tried to discover what made him swim; whatever he tried to do in the water, he always kept afloat.

Again, from my interrogations of physicists, engineers, and bicycle manufacturers, I have come to the conclusion that the principle by which the cyclist keeps his balance is not generally known. The rule observed by the cyclist is this. When he starts falling to the right he turns the handlebars to the right, so that the course of the bicycle is deflected along a curve towards the right. This results in a centrifugal force pushing the cyclist to the left and offsets the gravitational force dragging him down to the right. This manoeuvre presently throws the cyclist out of balance to the left, which he counteracts by turning the handlebars to the left; and so he continues to keep himself in balance by winding along a series of appropriate curvatures. A simple analysis shows that for a given angle of unbalance the curvature of each winding is inversely proportional to the square of the speed at which the cyclist is proceeding.

But does this tell us exactly how to ride a bicycle? No. You obviously cannot adjust the curvature of your bicycle's path in proportion to the ratio of your unbalance over the square of your speed; and if you could you would fall off the machine, for there are a number of other factors to be taken into account in practice which are left out in the formulation of this rule. Rules of art can be useful, but they do not determine the practice of an art; they are maxims, which can serve as a guide to an art only if they can be integrated into the practical knowledge of the art. They cannot replace this knowledge.

MICHAEL POLANYI

**One last question: All this sounds very
nice, but so many students don't seem to
know how to really read a text.**

It depends upon what one means by *really read*. People often use the phrase *really read* to mean that students do not come up with their particular "reading" of a text. Students do not see the same things teachers see, and they do not see them the same way. Surely out of five billion responses the teacher's response is not superior to *any* other response.

But, if one means by *really read*, students do not pay attention to all the verbal details that produce their general responses, there is a grain of truth. People who respond to Picasso's *Guernica* don't pay attention to the strength and direction of the brushstrokes. Many people who respond fully to a symphony do not pay attention to what key it's in. The comment might mean people who read poems are not professionals.

We expect people to be highly attentive readers, though, because they read so much, and because they take twelve years of English. And they are more attentive than we give them credit for, but they are not used to explaining all the processes by which they come to like or dislike, interpret, evaluate, or make some other summative judgment about what they have read. There remains a question as to whether they need to or not. If you let a group of people talk about a poem for an hour without directing them in any way, you will find that collectively they touch upon most of the verbal details that produce the various general impressions. There is no need to lecture them on all these details or to hold a recitation.

The students do know how to *really read*; give them a chance to prove it.

THE
STRUCTURE OF THE
CLASSROOM

"The teacher teaches; the student learns. It's as simple as that!" so say proponents of the old kind of formal education that concentrates on teaching *things* instead of letting students learn and enjoy the learning. And letting students learn is what the response-centered curriculum is all about, since at its core is the idea that learning is a personal matter. It's a curriculum that enables the student to use his own senses and to trust them, to become alert to his own feelings, perceptions, interests, and own directions.

In Salinger's story "Teddy," Teddy, the doomed child genius, responds to the question, "What would you do if you could change the educational system?" by saying that he would not start with what schools generally do. He suggests meditation and the "real way of looking at things."

The real way of looking at things, according to Teddy, is to insist upon your own creative perceptions of experience in contrast to what he calls "apple-eaters," those who abide by conventional, worn perceptions. The difference is one between genuine personal response and experience, and conformism.

Teddy would not tell students how anything looks — then they would expect it to look that way.

This demand to see things the real way, the only way possible if it's going to mean anything to the individual, is a challenge for the classroom of the seventies in a response-centered curriculum. It is a challenge to provide literature to students in the hopes that they will exclaim, "I looked upon the world and saw it with my own eyes, as if they were the very first eyes that ever did see!"

What the classroom should BE like

To the traditionalists, the classroom of the response-centered curriculum may appear noisy, chaotic, and unstructured. Traditional rows of nailed-down desks have been replaced by chairs or desks in a variety of formations. Instead of students staring at the backs of other students, they now look at one another in the sharing of responses. They may look boldly. They may look defiantly. They may look pleadingly. Still, they look at the listener and communicate in a more natural dialogue of speaker to listener.

On one day, following the reading of Flannery O'Connor's "Everything That Rises Must Converge," some students may be grouped together to discuss the concept of racism in relation to the mother while others may be preparing to act out the scene between the Black child and the mother on the bus. Two students may be in a corner getting into the minds and hearts of Julian and his mother. Some others may be working independently on activities such as paintings which translate a particular facet of understanding for them — in this case, the paintings could capture the significance of the duplication of hats on the Black woman and the mother. Some others may be reading correlated materials, such as Lowenfels's "The Last Echo" or Greenburg's How to Be a Jewish Mother, or listening to related recordings, or viewing a film or filmstrip.

Some students may be writing a poem or an essay as an outpouring of their response to "Everything That Rises Must Converge." Still others may move freely from one activity to another as befits their learning styles, demands, and interests.

On another day, the class may regroup in a circle to involve all students in a discussion of Oedipus Rex, with particular reference to the allusion of the Oedipus Complex. Later, a few students may leave the group and quietly contemplate the impact of the drama on them. In the silence of their thoughts they may let the literature take hold of them completely in a way that has meaning for them.

It's curious. At one time, some teachers became alarmed at periods of silence in the classroom after they had asked a question that received no verbal student response. Yet, if the response to literature is personal, then a significant learning style is through self-communion and meditation.

In meditation, the student communes with himself, following the dictates of his own senses in the solitary search for personal meaning and substance of the literature. The student could be unraveling in his own mind the essence of *Oedipus Rex* in relation to him, his world, his experiences. At any rate, he gives way to the infusion of images and thoughts and sounds and shapes until dimensions emerge for more intensive explorations. It is at this point that the student may want to tape his thoughts and feelings before embarking on activities related to his response to *Oedipus Rex*.

No fixed plan exists in this class, since it is not static. It reflects the dynamism in the creative energies of students who themselves determine the kinds of activities that will help them work out their interaction with literature.

Real education, after all, is not something engendered by the other apple-eaters; it is within the individual student's corpus of abilities, potentials, and preferences. It is within his own person when he encounters the text and the encounter causes him to search, inquire, be curious, and hone his knowledge, understanding, and interest. Indeed, when he perceives it as real, a book is more than a book. It is rather a meeting that has meaning for him, that catapults him as an individual and sustains him as a unique being.

In the encounter between reader and text, vibrant things happen when students delight in reading and in sharing with one another experiences, ideas, and feelings

and

when what they learn involves a variety of different kinds of behaviors and experiences that exceed the mere acquisition of facts:

Reflecting   Solving problems
              Observing
                              Generating new ideas
      Exploring
                      Experimenting
                                      Developing concepts

Developing insights
                      Developing curiosity

                                      Forming generalizations
      Searching for relationships and analogies

This is not to say that facts have a negative value, but facts in themselves have only a temporary use in the process by which the individual acquires ideas. As isolated memorized and repeated items, facts do little to involve the student and to guide him in his intimate meeting with literature.

In what may seem to be a disconcerting classroom because there are no formulas, no authority figure telling students what to do, how to do it, and when, amazing things take place — simultaneously: learning and enjoyment!

In their own way, students are responding to literature according to what interests them, what meets their needs at the moment, what expands their experiences, and what touches their feelings about themselves and others. As a result of their involvement, perception, interpretation, and evaluation, students reach an understanding about literature and make it their own for life.

In their response, they are meeting the mind and heart of the artist firsthand and are facing the challenge confidently. They are also demonstrating that learning is something which involves both the senses and the intellect, and proving that individuals learn for themselves when they have a personal stimulus and an appropriate setting.

A DICTIONARY of LITERARY TERMS

XXIV (1959), 418-425.

oduces **rhythm**, recurrences at equal interval,
m a Greek word meaning "flow") is usually applied to
than feet. Often depends most obviously on pauses.
em with run-on ve a different rhythm from
h end-stopped oth are in the same
d prose, thou rhythm is
dition to bei
y pauses d
lysyllabic w
ords, even
hm is alte
ronuncia'
verbatim,
of the final line
the line before, even throug
ntical, as in Frost's "Stopping by

ERISM: The accidental reversal of sounds, especi
nds, of words, as in "poured with rain" for "roarec
." The term has immortalized the Rev. W. A. Spooner of
w College, Oxford, who was much given to such slips.
NG RHYTHM: As described by Gerard Manley Hopkins in his
ace to *Poems* (1876-1889), sprung rhythm is measured by
of from one to four syllables; however, any num-
bles may be used for special e
OVISM: See DOLCE STIL NUOVO.
AND TYPE CHARACTER: A stock character is a familiar figure
appears regularly in certain literary forms. Among the

syllable ending the run-on line receives only a light metrical
as on such words as "and," "if," "in"), it is a weak ending.
rung rhythm (a term coined by Gerard Manley Hopkins)
as one stressed syllable, which begins the foot, and any
of unstressed syllables. Note how the following lines (in an
given by Hopkins) each have three stressed syllables, but
umbers of unstressed ones.

Ding, | dong, | bell;
Pussy's | in the | well;
Who | put her | in?
Little | Johnny | Thin.

A Reader's Guide to LITERARY TERMS

ONOMATOPOEIA:

René Wellek and
Brace and Wo

A synonym for *stanza* (q.v.).
YTHIA: Greek: *stichos*, "a line"; *mythos*, "speech." Ih
dialogue consisting of single lines spoken alternately by
racters. Generally a verbal duel, stichomythia is charac-
by repetitive patterns and antithesis, as in these lines
mlet. Act III. Scene iv:
Both of the follow

True ease in writing come
As those move easiest who have

A run-on line has its sense carried over into the next line without
syntactical pause. This running-over is also kno as **enjambment.**

At the round earth's imagined cor
Your trumpets, angels. (Donne)

hree, four,
ock at the door;
e, six,
up sticks . . .

deism. See
denotation. See *connotation.
denouement. See *plot.

deus ex machina. Literally, a god from a
In Greek drama a god who descends by a crane-like an
solves a problem in the story, thus allowing the play t
unexpected and improbable device (e.g., an unexpec

THE LANGUAGE OF POETRY

Before going on to discuss
consider briefly a much more complicated distinction tha
ne between poetry and verse.
Here again the notion we have borrowed from Coleridge and
les valuable insight. To say that in poetry the
tention to itself is to suggest that
merely the *means* by
prose;
ee throug

CANSO: (Also *chanson*)
ORATION: A formal address

The textual critic is perhaps better named the text
He seeks to establish the proper text for study, and thus
by knowledge and reasoning whether, for example, Har
(according to the various printed texts) his "solid flesh"
flesh" or "sallied flesh" to melt. (Consult *F. Bowers, 7
Literary Criticism.) "Te criticism," in an entire
sense, has occasionally the **new criticism,** a sc
name was probab Crowe Ransom's book
Criticis " is commonly appl
th Brooks, Robert
Ransom himsel

To put of sty-
s of the oetry of the
ue"; fo which, incider
nguage is yday conversation on the
of prose s uality of standard journalistic
utely free of an s an area where poetry and prose
istic contrivanc some pieces of prose are genuinely
densest and mos poems, or parts of poems, seem hardly
tally, come from al s one had better be content to say simply
to both the s tend to make more use of "poetry" than prose does.
nd and i the c

IMAGES AND FIGURES OF SPEECH—
THE CONCRETE AND THE ANALOGICAL IN POETRY

ma nguage which
another that seeks to convey one world by
figuration—that is, the
It should be added that poetry often

onstitute
tedly its
poetry
s par-
world of eye

I presume not God to scan;
kind/ is Man. (Pope)
syntactical pause.
VERSE, POETRY, AND PROSE—SOME DISTINCTIONS

hance, (Pope)
to dance. (Pope)

VIRELAY: (Also French, *virelai*). A name applied to either of t
verse forms, neither of which is strictly fixed, derived from c
French poetry. One, used for a poem of limited length, has on
two rhymes; the first and second lines appear alternately as
frains. The other has an indefinite number of stanzas, ea
having two rhymes, one rhyme in long lines, the other in sho

ROYAL, SPENSERIAN STANZA. See also VERSE PARAGRAPH,
STASIMON: 1. A term used by I. A. Richards in hi
criticism to indicate scientifically verifiable s
STATEMENT: 1. A division of a se
STATEMENT:

ONTOLOGY: See STRU
OPEN COUPLET: A co

The classroom is a collage of activities, a forum for the exchange of ideas, a place of intellectual interplay between student and text, between student and student, and between student and teacher. The challenge is endless.

In the meantime, where is the teacher and what is he doing? He is there; yet he is not there in the traditional sense.

No longer the authority figure in front of the class engaging in constant "talk-talk," the teacher stimulates, challenges, and goads when necessary.

He moves from one group to another, from one student to another and reaches out to each one.

He suggests rather than tells, demonstrates rather than lectures.

Most important, as he circulates around the room, he asks questions that challenge students to reach beyond their grasp and to explore alternatives.

He is a devil's advocate when the occasion demands it, a facilitator, a mediator, a LISTENER.

He establishes an atmosphere in the classroom where disagreements and personal conflicts are considered in an atmosphere of mutual respect, where interactions among students are high, and where each individual is treated with dignity.

He stresses synthesis rather than analysis of ideas; exploration and discovery of new ideas rather than a refinement of previously discovered areas.

He insists that students be responsible for supporting what they say as they examine themselves, their world, and their literature.

He establishes challenging situations as a basis for stimulating students.

He permits students to "put things together for themselves, to be their own discoverers."

He receives and reacts quickly to nonverbal messages which students emit with their own private codes.

He creates a climate and offers resources and opportunities in which individual understanding grows and is directed from within.

He prizes students as individuals; he is aware of and values their feelings and thoughts.

He conveys genuine concern and understanding based on students' own perceptions and accepts their way of perceiving and relating to life in the classroom.

He is creative and has these characteristics   sensitive to others

            observant   honest

knowledgeable   helpful   resourceful

               intuitive

    open-minded

What the classroom should FEEL like

Initially, students may experience some frustration in the response-centered curriculum, if for no other reason than they have not been accustomed to the teacher's asking them, "What do you think?" They have not been used to being listened to and acknowledged when they express what they think.

They have, in fact, been accustomed to being maneuvered and programmed toward values and goals that appear to be their own, until they delude themselves into thinking that they really are their own.

They have been dehumanized to the point where skills and subject matter have been more important than they are; where courses and objectives must be followed regardless of the students' wishes, capacities, and interests; and where explaining and analyzing supplant spontaneity and feeling.

In the long run, students shun school and, specifically,

the teacher who prepares lessons mechanically, specifying the number of pages to be covered and the questions to be answered

the teacher who stresses subject over learner

the teacher who concentrates exclusively on facts and details, right and wrong answers,

Like the classroom of "M'Choakumchild's Schoolroom" that Dickens described in *Hard Times*:

Now, what I want is Facts. Teach these boys and girls nothing but Facts. Facts alone are wanted in life. Plant nothing else, and root out everything else. You can only form the minds of reasoning animals upon Facts: nothing else will ever be of any service to them.

Gradually, however, students become creative and free with a full realization that their individuality and uniqueness are valued, respected, and trusted. They realize that they can explore and respond to literature in relation to themselves, their world, and their interests, potentials, and experiences.

The classroom should have the feeling of a oneness with the individual and his interactions to other students and the teacher. An inviting warmth pervades the classroom, enticing students into the family of the class.

What should BE in this classroom?

movable chairs   bookcases   worktables   a lot of paperback books   chalkboards   files of photographs and magazine clippings   a screen   shades to darken the room   bulletin boards

THESE ARE MUSTS

television monitor   typewriter   tape recorder   record player   projector (8mm. Super 8; *or* 16 mm. — all, if you can)   slide projector   overhead projector

THESE ARE IMPORTANT

videotape recorder   film library   mimeograph   copying equipment   opaque projector   slide, tape, book collections

THESE YOU SHOULD HAVE ACCESS TO

It is a classroom where the student feels

that the teacher values and accepts him as a whole person

that he is profoundly and actively involved in his own life and the life of the class as well

that he can fully respond to literature and meditate on his responses

that he has material with which to express himself

that he is experiencing excitement and joy in learning

that he is not in competition with other students

that he is free to extend the challenge to his potential as far as possible

that he learns not only from his experiences with other students, but from his own resources as well

that the teacher is no longer the sole individual on whom he must rely for help

that he becomes more independent as a learner and more functional as a person

that he develops an inquiring mind

Students know intuitively when they have a teacher who is sincere in his concern for them as individuals. Similarly, they know when they are in a classroom where the atmosphere is one of acceptance and respect. This knowledge on the part of students, perhaps more than any other, is essential, for they are the ones who are the inheritors of the dream and who somehow make it all worthwhile.

Just as a poem *becomes* even in the process of writing, so a response-centered classroom *becomes* even in the process of its being established. It is a step to a new creation, enabling all students to interact with an author, with literature, and with their world. In this creative setting, anything is possible.

TALK IN
THE CLASSROOM

There are certain experiences in life which must be shared in order to be appreciated. Just as it takes two to tango, it takes two to enjoy a good dinner or to see a good movie. It takes two to have a good cry or a good laugh, to exult or to grieve. (No doubt your imagination will provide other examples of activities that are enhanced when shared.)

And for most students in school, it takes two (or more) to read a piece of literature.

When we see a play or a film or a painting that stirs us, we are almost compelled to talk to someone about it. If we gain an insight, we want to share it. If we're puzzled, we want to ask questions. If we feel, but don't know how we feel, we want to hear how others respond. For most people this kind of talk is both essential and pleasurable.

**And for most students in school, talking about what
they read may be more important than the act of reading itself.**

When adults are deprived of an opportunity to talk, to share, to communicate a response to an experience, the result may be nothing more than a slightly irritating frustration. No matter how acute this feeling may be, it passes in time with little or no permanent damage. Adults have many opportunities to share their perceptions and intuitions about esthetic experiences, and for them a few denials will not be traumatic.

**But for most students in school, the continued lack
of opportunity to talk about the things they read will result
in a loss of interest in literature, a diminution of creative
imagination, and a hostility toward reading of any kind.**

Desire for knowledge, at any rate for a good deal of knowledge, is natural to the young, but is generally destroyed by the fact that they are given more than they desire or can assimilate. Children who are forced to eat acquire a loathing for food, and children who are forced to learn acquire a loathing for knowledge. When they think, they do not think spontaneously in the way in which they run or jump or shout: they think with a view to pleasing some adult, and therefore with an attempt at correctness rather than from natural curiosity. The killing of spontaneity is especially disastrous in artistic directions. Children who are taught literature or painting or music to excess, or with a view to correctness rather than to self-expression, become progressively less interested in the esthetic side of life.

BERTRAND RUSSELL

*Don't most English teachers encourage
their pupils to talk about the things
they read?*

Not according to a recent study.* Students throughout the country
reported that their teachers used the following approaches, listed in order
of frequency, when presenting a poem to the class:

explication or analysis
study of theme
discussion
reading aloud
study of technical aspects
listening to recordings
study of poets' lives
writing a poem
writing an analysis
oral interpretation
memorization
comparing of poems
also outlining, précis writing, research, a study of the point
of view, meter, use of study guides, etc.

Ask yourself how many of these approaches are teacher centered.
How many are pupil centered? Are any response centered?
Another study showed that teachers spend most of their time holding
recitations.

* James R. Squire and Roger K. Applebee, A Study of English Programs in Selected High
Schools Which Consistently Educate Outstanding Students in English, New York, 1968.

*Why is it so important for kids to talk
about the things they read?*

Suppose, for a moment, that you're a student in a tenth-grade English class, and that your teacher has handed out a ditto sheet containing this poem by Emily Dickinson.

PEDIGREE

**The pedigree of honey
Does not concern the bee;
A clover, any time, to him
Is aristocracy.**

You read the poem silently and then the teacher starts a lesson. Most of the time the teacher talks, but occasionally she asks a question. You hear all about:

the life of Emily Dickinson
the meaning of *pedigree*
the meaning of *aristocracy*
the central metaphor of the poem
the subordinate images and symbols
the speaker in the poem
the rhyme scheme of the poem
the meter of the poem
the development of the quatrain in English and American literature
the message of the poem
the evils of prejudice

For the students who remain awake and alert throughout this lecture, the lesson may or may not turn out to be a rewarding experience. Probably how much they remember will depend to a great extent on the dynamism of the teacher and the fact that they're having a test on Friday. However, their lives will most likely be unaffected, except in the most trivial way, by what they have read or heard during that class. They may *know* more when they get through, but they will not *be* more.

Now, let's look at another teacher. Instead of lecturing, this teacher hands out the poem and waits for something to happen. For a while it may look as if nothing is going on, but you *know* that ideas, feelings, tentative thoughts, and half-formulated responses are churning around and clicking away, and that questions and conclusions are slowly (or quickly) popping to the surface inside thirty brains. Here, the teacher does not lecture, but a lot of other things may take place:

The teacher may read the poem aloud or ask if someone wants to do it.

A student may ask the meaning of a difficult word. Someone else may answer or offer to look it up.

A boy may say the poem is stupid and makes no sense.

Another may say it's about bees and that he doesn't like bees.

A girl may say that she doesn't know what the poem means but that she likes the way it sounds.

The teacher may ask her why.

A boy may claim that he could write a better poem than that.

A student may say that he doesn't think the poem is about bees at all.

A small disagreement may emerge about whether or not the poem deals with bees.

The teacher may show the class a picture or have them improvise a play.

A youngster may say that he doesn't like the rhythm of the poem, that it's too much *dum-da-dum-da-dum*, too sing-songy.

The teacher may have it be read aloud again, perhaps by several readers.

The teacher may suggest that the class break up into small groups to talk about the poem.

Which of those is a better lesson?

In the first lesson the boys and girls (learn, listen to, are exposed to) a lot of important information about a poem and about the art of poetry. They remain largely unchanged by the experience.

In the second lesson the class may appear to be learning a lot less, but in reality they are gaining much more. In this kind of "open," seemingly unstructured experience they are learning:

a that their own responses have validity and that they are taken seriously by others, including adults,

b that there are others who share their responses,

c that there are others whose responses may be quite different from theirs,

d that all of these responses are legitimate and acceptable,

and

e that by talking about a poem they can add new dimensions to their original responses and learn new ways of responding.

Isn't there a middle ground, something less extreme, halfway between the lecture and the response-centered curriculum?

In many school systems the developmental (sometimes called socratic) literature lesson has served well for sizable numbers of the student population. But the problem with the developmental lesson is that it originates from a teacher's preconception of what a work means, how it is to be interpreted, and how youngsters should feel about it. The plan of a typical developmental lesson is really a script with the teacher's lines (usually questions) included and the students' lines (usually answers) omitted. It has a specific aim, a specific conclusion, a specific direction.

What's wrong with this approach?

It is not "wrong"; it's just limited. It has its place, but it is simply inadequate. We know that there are thousands of ways of responding to a work of literature, not just one. We know that very often the pupil has as interesting ideas as the teacher. We know that sometimes the best experiences in life are unpredictable. We know that if a student's imagination is to be set free, it cannot be programmed either by a computer or by a lesson plan.

Isn't there a chance that pupils will not respond at all when you approach the teaching of literature in this open way?

Yes, and that's a chance you'll have to take. The students may not want to say anything after they read a poem or a story. You may then decide to let it go at that and go on to something else. (This act takes courage, especially the first time.) Or, you may feel that the class needs a little help in getting started. In that case you will probably want to develop a small repertoire of pump-priming, more or less nondirective questions or devices.

Well?

How about that?

Billy? (Rising inflection here.)

Hm-m. (Teacher looks puzzled.)

What do you think?

Do you like that?

In addition, for some selections it will be necessary to conduct a brief discussion or conversation prior to reading the piece. The decision to do this would depend on many factors, including the complexity of the selection or its remoteness from the students' world of experience.

But if no one has anything to offer, you may simply read the piece again. Or ask the class why they're not saying anything. Or, the most nerve-wracking technique of all, do or say nothing. How long can the class hold out before someone ventures a comment? The pressure can be awesome.

One point must be made. It is those groups that seem to respond least who need this approach most. There are many classes in countless schools where youngsters have been taught that they are there to listen and to learn. After years of this sort of passive attention-paying and avid note-taking, followed by giving it all back on climactic tests, it's no wonder that these students have little confidence in their own responses, in their own intuitions and evaluations. It's these tightly wired-up students who can be the primary beneficiaries of a response-centered approach. Of course, it will take longer to get them to respond freely, will be harder for them to abandon their accustomed roles in the paternalistic school structure; but it's doubtful that time could be better spent.

> Can you PROVE, in black and white, that this
> kind of free unstructured talk is better for students
> than either the lecture or the developmental lesson?

Honestly, realistically, scientifically, no — at least, not entirely. We do know that relaxed teachers do better than authoritarian ones. And there is ample evidence, scientific and otherwise, that the traditional methods of teaching literature have failed for millions of boys and girls. Ask yourself whether these traditional approaches have produced a general populace that is interested in reading good literature. Do most people go on reading after their formal education is concluded, do they move freely in worlds of creativity and imagination?

The aim of education is not storing the Mind with the various sorts of knowledge most in request, as if the Human Soul were a mere repository or banqueting room, but to please it in such relations of circumstance as should gradually excite its vegetating and germinating powers to produce new fruits of Thought, new Conceptions, and Imaginations, and Ideas.

SAMUEL TAYLOR COLERIDGE

Does a teacher have to do any planning in a response-centered approach, or does he simply go to the room, hand out material, and play it by ear?

This may discourage you, but the teacher frequently has to do more intensive planning when working with responses than he would have to do if he were lecturing or using the developmental approach. But it's planning of an entirely different kind. Instead of facts or questions, the plan consists of:

alternatives

options   *suggestions*

possibilities

strategies   *problems*

expectations

playing it by ear

Can you provide a specific example of how this would work?

Let's suppose you were going to teach this poem.

TRAVELING THROUGH THE DARK

Traveling through the dark I found a deer
dead on the edge of the Wilson River road.
It is usually best to roll them into the canyon:
that road is narrow; to swerve might make more dead.

By glow of tail-light I stumbled back of the car
and stood by the heap, a doe, a recent killing;
she had stiffened already, almost cold.
I dragged her off; she was big in the belly.

My fingers touching her side brought me the reason;
her side was warm; her fawn lay there waiting,
alive, still, never to be born.
Beside that mountain road I hesitated.

The car aimed ahead its lowered parking lights;
under the hood purred the steady engine.
I stood in the glare of the warm exhaust turning red;
around our group I could hear the wilderness listen.

I thought hard for us all — my only swerving —
then pushed her over the edge into the river.

WILLIAM STAFFORD

You will probably want to read this poem several times, and then jot down or think through your own reactions and responses. This is a necessary first step before presenting a poem to a class. Your thoughts on the poem might run something like this, though bear in mind that this is just *one* way of responding, and that it need not be yours.

I like the poem. It's tightly constructed — it all fits together — and it makes me feel sad. But it's a good feeling of sadness, not depression, because my insight into the human condition is enhanced by it. It's a statement about the tragedy of death-in-life put in terms of strong, clear images. By the end of the poem I am the live fawn in the dead doe hurtling through the darkness toward the river. And the whole scene is very vivid. I can picture the tableau with that eerie tail-light turning the smoke red. And the purring of the car's engine, is that the relentlessness of life itself? The tone of the poem is good, too — natural and conversational, yet dealing with the mysterious and the infinite. A man is telling his friends of a recent experience, and he's trying to see some meaning in what he has just seen and done, and to understand how it all made him feel. Stafford's use of that line

I thought hard for us all — my only swerving —

makes the poem a universal statement, instead of just a personal one. And the ending of the poem brings me back to the beginning, to the title. Am I the one who is traveling through the dark? Is it the poet? The doe? The fawn? Everybody?

Now that you know more about how you feel about the poem, you can consider the question of how to treat it in class. How will your students respond to it? What problems might they have with it? What will they like? What will they dislike? How will it make them feel?

As has been mentioned earlier, often it is a good practice to conduct some talk prior to reading a work. The idea here is to facilitate the ability of the students to become sensitive and receptive to whatever they're going to read. It's getting them in the mood. To help them feel the subtle power of "Traveling Through the Dark," you might talk about these questions, or others like them, before the class looks at the work:

Do you think that, in general, people like animals? Why?

Suppose that you saw a dead robin or other bird on your lawn. What would be your reaction?

What would your reaction be if the bird were seriously injured, but still alive?

Would your feeling be the same if the animal were not a bird, but a squirrel, or a cat, or a dog?

During this kind of classroom talk you should try to keep from commenting on their responses. Simply let the students react to the questions and to one another. Then, when they have had ample opportunity to explain their attitudes about animals and about death, read the poem aloud. The transition from the pre-reading discussion to the oral reading should be kept very simple. It should not be devious, clever or elaborate. It should be an invitation, something like:

Well, let's see what you think of the attitudes expressed by the writer of this poem.

You might then read the poem aloud while the pupils follow from their own copies. You could start the flow of talk with questions like these:

How did the poem make you feel?

What made you feel that way?

With a group accustomed to this method, the responses might start coming without any cue from you.

It is no doubt desirable for the teacher to be sensitive to student responses. But the teacher should not express value judgments or engage in heavy-handed probing or analysis, for this will surely impede or inhibit the free flow of response.

When the students have expressed their feelings about the poem, you could ask them:

Just who is it that's traveling through the dark?

*And what is **the dark,** anyway?*

One sure way to elicit student response is to ask one member of the class to assume the place of the driver of the car and to tell the class of his experience. Ask him to explain what went on in his mind between his finding the dead deer and his disposing of the body. The class could ask him questions, and then they could react to what he had said.

Do you sense that the youngsters want to talk more about the poem? You could keep the conversation going by the use of questions such as these:

What do you think the title of the poem means?

Do you ever travel through the dark? When?

What do you think the poet means in saying, "I thought hard for us all."? Who is us all?

Why are we involved in the situation? ("I thought hard for us all.") Are we part of the group in line 16?

Why, in your opinion, did the driver of the car hesitate before he pushed the doe off the road? Do you think that this hesitation was his "only swerving"?

How would you describe the mood of the poem? What expressions or images help create that mood?

What is the effect of the unusual word order ending the first line and beginning the second?

There are many other activities that could conceivably grow out of a discussion of the kind pictured here. Some of these other ways of responding are dealt with in detail in other portions of this book.

*What is the precise role of the teacher
in this sort of conversation about
literature?*

The teacher chooses material which he thinks will be interesting, important, and exciting to his pupils.

The teacher learns to respond freely to a work of literature.

The teacher analyzes his own response.

The teacher tries to anticipate some of the ways his pupils might respond.

The teacher designs several alternate ways of presenting the selection.

The teacher plans questions aimed at eliciting response.

The teacher plans questions aimed at broadening the response.

The teacher plans activities aimed at eliciting and broadening response.

The teacher pre-selects other works of literature to which the class might
turn.

The teacher learns to take his cues from what the pupils are saying, as
well as from what they're not saying.

The teacher learns to subordinate his own role.

**Teachers seem to assume that they play the starring role in the kids' lives. What
rubbish that is. To many of the kids, school doesn't even exist, except as a place
where you've got to go to stay out of trouble. Or to get warm. Or to pick up girls.**

SUNNY DECKER

*Does the teacher have to adopt a new
personality?*

It is quite possible that the teacher may have to work toward a new
persona, if not a new personality. Obviously a teacher can no longer be
authoritarian. He cannot be rigid, and he cannot promote — either con-
sciously or unconsciously — the notion that he knows all the answers. Nor
can he promote the notion that works of literature are religious relics. He
cannot be a judge of pupil responses, but instead a keen elicitor and auditor. He must be largely nondirective in his approach.

The teacher must convince his students that he is — more than anything else — interested in the way they feel about the things they read. He
must convince them that they do not have to like everything they read.
The students have to be made to feel that they can reject a poem without
rejecting their teacher. If they don't like the anthology they have, they
should assemble their own.

*In what way are the questions asked by
teachers using the response-centered
approach different from those
customarily posed by teachers of
their students?*

Although there are many similarities, there are also significant differences. Response-centered talk is primarily initiated by questions for
which there are no correct answers. The traditional question-and-answer
recitation has no place in this method. Instead of merely calling for facts,
the questions call for opinions, feelings, reactions, ideas, responses.

Even the technique of posing the question is somewhat different. For
example, if you were teaching "Traveling Through the Dark," to ask

What went on in the man's mind?

would presuppose or imply that there is a known answer. To open up the question (and, it is hoped, the student), better phrasing would be

What do you think went on in his mind?

This is not a minor or unimportant distinction. The former question tends to shut out all those who are unsure; the latter invites all to share what they feel. Compare, if you will, these two columns:

TRADITIONAL	RESPONSE-CENTERED
What does the title mean?	What do you think the title means?
Who is the speaker in the poem?	Do you have a picture in your mind of the speaker in this poem? What is it?
Is this a Shakespearian or a Petrarchan sonnet?	Do you like the way this poem is written? Why?

Once the pupils start talking, what does the teacher do?

He listens very carefully (those porcupines again).

And what does that mean?

The teacher must feign, if he really doesn't feel, a kind of innocence when the kids start talking. He has really got to pretend that he hasn't studied English literature for five years at a leading university. He has got to try to see the work through the eyes of a child, and he must never express disapproval, disbelief, disdain, or dismay. The integrity of the students' responses must be preserved.

The pinnacle of this kind of ingenuous dissembling is reached when the pupils feel that they are teaching the teacher, when they try to bridge the "generation gap."

In addition to maintaining the open quality of this approach while the talk is going on, the teacher listens attentively to determine the direction of the talk:

Who's doing most of the talking?

Who is not participating?

What problems do they seem to be having with the work?

What activities might tie in with what they're saying?

What other works could they read to add another dimension to their understanding and appreciation?

What do they seem to be leaving out of their talk?

What can I do to get them to talk more to each other?

What additional questions can I ask to make them aware of other ways of responding?

Are some responses better than others?

While on the one hand it is counterproductive to place a value judgment on pupils' responses, it is important at the same time to realize that there are many kinds of responses, and that one of the goals of this program is to broaden the students' responses — in effect, to make them aware that there is more than one way of responding to a work of literature.

In general, there are four areas of response:

a Engagement-Involvement. *On this level the reader becomes subjectively involved in the work. This is the affective response, the one in which the youngster feels, or does not feel, identification or empathy.*

b Perception. *On this level the reader views the work objectively. Perception means seeing a selection as a product of human creation rather than as a natural phenomenon.*

c Interpretation. *The reader may use either subjective or objective viewpoints in seeking to tell what the work means. Interpretation is translation of metaphor.*

d Evaluation. *On this level the reader, using either subjective or objective criteria, seeks to compare this work with others and to assess its impact and importance.*

Most of us begin by being involved in what we read and then, possibly, continue into one or more of the other three areas. Engagement is perhaps the least sophisticated way of responding, and evaluation is the most. One is not better than the other, but they are not the same.

In your careful attention to your youngsters' talk about the things they read, you may notice a tendency on the part of some to limit their responses to one of the four areas, while more or less excluding the others. For example, a student may restrict his comments to interpreting what he has read. (Unfortunately, many students are trained to read poetry in this manner exclusively.) Another may like to talk primarily in terms of evaluating the selections he reads. In cases like these, you will want to ask questions that will make the pupils aware of the other areas of response.

Since there is a kind of structure inherent in this overview of response patterns, you will probably want to keep these levels in mind when you do your initial planning. Generally speaking, most talk about literature — and particularly with younger students — should start on the level of engagement-involvement. It should go on to include perception, interpretation, and evaluation, not necessarily in that order, and not usually in equal amounts. Discussions never really end, though they may be set aside temporarily to go on to other activities; or they may return to their starting points as a way of determining the extent of growth or change.

Let's assume that your group is working with this poem:

ON A SQUIRREL CROSSING THE ROAD IN
AUTUMN, IN NEW ENGLAND

It is what he does not know,
Crossing the road under the elm trees,
About the mechanism of my car,
About the Commonwealth of Massachusetts,
About Mozart, India, Arcturus,

That wins my praise. I engage
At once in whirling squirrel-praise.

He obeys the orders of nature
Without knowing them.
It is what he does not know
That makes him beautiful.
Such a knot of little purposeful nature!

I who can see him as he cannot see himself
Repose in the ignorance that is his blessing,

It is what man does not know of God
Composes the visible poem of the world.
          . . . . . Just missed him!

                    RICHARD EBERHART

Before the class reads the poem, you might want to establish receptivity and sensitivity by posing questions such as these:

What thoughts or feelings do you have when you see an animal run across the road in front of your car, bus, or bicycle?

Does any part of you want to kill him?

Have *you* ever run in front of a moving vehicle? How did you feel?

Do you suppose that an animal in such a situation has similar feelings?

After they've talked and argued, you read the poem. The kids are excited. They want to talk about the poem now. Here are some of their comments:

The squirrel doesn't know that he could get killed by the car. He is just running across the road.

The poet says that it's what he doesn't know that makes him beautiful.

You mean that ignorance is bliss.

The driver knows all about those complicated things like Mozart and Arcturus — what's Arcturus? — and that's why he's superior to the squirrel.

Who said he's superior? The squirrel is better off than the driver.

Do you mean that you'd rather be a squirrel?

No, I don't. What I mean is that the man knows about the beauty of life, but he also knows about death. He knows about suffering and about horror, and the squirrel doesn't, and that's why the squirrel is better off.

This is by no means an uninteresting discussion. The students have been able, on their own, to isolate an issue of importance to them, and they are talking about it with intelligence and maturity. All of their comments so far, however, have to do with interpretation. They are exploring the metaphor, telling what they think the poem means. This is fine, but you may want to broaden their response by directing their energy and attention to the other three areas. You might very well want to ask questions such as these:

To further engagement and involvement:

When you read the poem, did you see the experience through the eyes of the squirrel, the driver, or neither?

Do you like the driver?

(Note: You may have noticed that the Eberhart poem bears certain similarities to Stafford's "Traveling Through the Dark." If the two poems were to be taught together, their juxtaposition might serve as an additional stimulus to student response. If that were the case, you could also ask these two questions.)

Do you think the same kind of man could have written both poems?

Can you compare your feelings after reading each of the two poems?

To further perception:

What do you think of the way this poem is written?

Do you find the title amusing? How about the last half-line? Do you suppose the author intended them to be amusing?

The poem states that the squirrel obeys the laws of nature without knowing them, and yet in another line he is called purposeful. Does this seem like a contradiction to you?

How much time elapses, do you think, from the beginning to the end of this incident? Is the poet successful, in your opinion, in conveying this rapid passage of time?

To further evaluation:

Do you think this is a good poem? Did you like it more or less than "Traveling Through the Dark"?

Do you agree or disagree with the poet's view of life?

Do you think the poem has any meaning for technological society?

Is it a better poem than Stafford's? More serious? Better written?

In this way you can fulfill your role as keen auditor. By taking your cues from what they say when they talk about literature, you can redress any imbalance in their approach to what they read.

Sample poetry lesson

PRE-READING CONVERSATION

(Use one or more of these questions to facilitate involvement in the poem.)

Many psychologists maintain that adolescence is the most difficult period in a person's life. It seems, also, that there are many teenagers who would just as soon skip the whole thing and go on to adulthood. Would you? Why?

Some movies and TV programs would have us believe that adolescence is a time of life that is free of responsibility and devoted entirely to the pursuit of pleasure. The typical TV teenager is not too bright and interested primarily in hamburgers, stereo sets, sportscars, and clothes. Do you think this is an accurate picture? Why?

Teenagers often accuse their parents and other adults of forgetting what it's like to be young. This may be true, of course, but how accurately can you remember what it was like to be eight or nine years old?

What do you like least about being a teenager? What most?

THE POEM

(Usually the initial reading of the poem will be done by the teacher.)

FIFTEEN

South of the bridge on Seventeenth
I found back of the willows one summer
day a motorcycle with engine running
as it lay on its side, ticking over
slowly in the high grass. I was fifteen.

I admired all that pulsing gleam, the
shiny flanks, the demure headlights
fringed where it lay; I led it gently
to the road and stood with that
companion, ready and friendly. I was fifteen.

We could find the end of a road, meet
the sky on out Seventeenth. I thought about
hills, and patting the handle got back a
confident opinion. On the bridge we indulged
a forward feeling, a tremble. I was fifteen.

Thinking, back farther in the grass I found
the owner, just coming to, where he had flipped
over the rail. He had blood on his hand, was pale —
I helped him walk to his machine. He ran his hand
over it, called me good man, roared away.

I stood there, fifteen.

WILLIAM STAFFORD

TALKING POINTS

(These questions, or others like them, may be used to get the discussion started, or to guide it in directions in which it does not seem to be going by itself.)

How did the poem make you feel?

How do you think the boy in the poem felt? At the beginning? At the end?

Have you ever felt as he did?

Why do you think the motorcycle meant so much to him?

Is it possible that the motorcycle stood for something else? What do you think?

The poem tells us four times that the boy was fifteen. Does this repetition have any effect on you? What? Is it the same effect each time?

If you were painting a picture of the poem, what split second would you try to capture in your painting? Why? Can you describe the colors you would use and the background of the scene

Do you like this poem? Why? Why not?

OUTREACH

(These suggestions for further activities could grow out of the talk in the classroom.)

The class might have a discussion on adult-teenager relationships. Beginning with the patronizing line of the poem, "He . . . called me good man," the group could consider other ways in which adults "put down" teen-

agers. Besides dwelling on the negative aspects of adult-adolescent relationships, the group might well consider what teenagers can do to improve these relationships.

Some students might want to try, after reading the poem, actually painting the scene they discussed.

Some might try creating a collage of pictures and designs reflecting the mood of the poem.

Some might do some imaginative writing based on finding the end of a road or meeting the sky.

Some might want to try to express the poem or its mood in music.

Some could write a play based on the incident.

Some could do anything they thought of, anything the poem made them want to do — something I cannot even visualize or imagine.

Some could do nothing.

The teacher might suggest other reading to the class such as other poems by William Stafford or works (of any genre) dealing with a sensitive adolescent's growing perception of his status as a second-class citizen in a world ruled by adults. The ambivalence of the adolescent is one of the most persistent themes of literature, and you are surely familiar with numerous examples of works dealing with the torments of teenagers torn between the childhood they haven't quite left, and the adulthood they have not yet attained. Nevertheless, these few personal examples may cause you to remember a few more.

J. D. SALINGER, Catcher in the Rye

JAMES T. FARRELL, The Danny O'Neill trilogy.

JAMES JOYCE, A Portrait of the Artist as a Young Man.

JOHN KNOWLES, A Separate Peace.

HARPER LEE, To Kill a Mockingbird.

Will the students make any progress under the response-centered approach, or will their taste always remain the same?

Taste is probably a product of opportunity, maturation, saturation, and self-confidence. In classes where pupils are encouraged to respond freely, honestly, and creatively to what they read, taste will grow. But the teacher cannot conduct himself as if his taste is superior, nor can he ever sneer at the taste of his pupils. He must provide opportunities for the pupils to read more, and he need not be concerned that this additional reading matter be of "literary" quality. An atmosphere of happy excitement and joyous enticement must prevail so that talk about literary works is not an end, but a beginning. Talk in the classroom must lead to more reading, as well as to the myriad other responses described in this book.

FILM AND OTHER MOVING MEDIA:

THAT'S GREAT... WHAT'S IT FOR?

School seldom teaches kids how to deal with their environment. Our students live in a visual, oral, nonprint, nonbook culture, they love visions and films and television and rock music — but they don't learn in school how to deal with the vast quantity of these things that surround them. As the visual, verbal, sensual world multiplies, we must help our students handle that environment and be able to recognize, expect, and demand value in it. Or else resign ourselves to a career of perpetuating mediocrity. We can't continue to teach our frozen curricula and turn our backs on our students' natural interests and influences — especially when they easily fit into our English classrooms.

Not that listening to rock music and making and viewing films and television should be all there is to English study. Paying some attention to moving media, integrating it into the English classroom doesn't mean abrogating the rest of literature — it means opening up "English" to the larger "universe of discourse." And the new media are so much a part of everyone's environment, are so easily obtained by the schools, and are even more easily operated, that it seems at the very least foolish to ignore the possibilities films, tapes, and records open up.

I don't mean use them in the way English classrooms have in the past — using records and tapes "to enhance" literature (How many of us have been subjected to hearing Vachel Lindsay read "The Congo"?). English teachers have also used films of literature, complete and excerpted sections of feature-length films, and films about the parts of speech and the library. But that is all. All the remaining technological products and possibilities have generally been ignored. Even when the schools began purchasing equipment such as tape recorders, record players, and cameras, the English classroom felt uncomfortable about it — "that's great . . . what's it for?" — and discarded the equipment or avoided full use of it.

So, through these technological years, the English classroom's sphere has remained generally unchanged, while outside the school students' experiences with the new symbolic, narrative, and factual environment has increased. Now, in the seventies, there is movement toward that wider definition of English and learning how to work with all the parts together — students with their teachers, all contributing their responses, knowledge, environments, and backgrounds to open up the English classroom so that it can accept all kinds of responses. This new direction assumes that teachers must learn to handle and view, no less than be aware of, their surroundings. We all need to be able to deal with taste and quality in our lives, and the only way is to expose ourselves and our students to enough stimuli and to begin to raise and educate expectations and desires — ours and theirs.

Since film is an active participant in both mass media and art, it is an excellent means to unite life, art, and school. The study of film, more than any other medium, closely parallels "standard" approaches to what is already studied in the English classroom — literature.

Film can be dealt with from two directions that are in themselves standard approaches — filmmaking and film study. Filmmaking typically generates from film study but can be used as a form of response in the English classroom, just as an essay or any student-created work is used.

Film study, which involves viewing, discussing, and responding to many films, fits naturally into the English classroom because films are, in a broad sense, literature. They concern narrative technique, conflict, point of view, theme, etc., as fiction or poetry or expository writing does. Film begins with an artist's perception as literature or any other art does, but it communicates that perception in a different form — a new technological form that shares terminology with the rest of the arts. Film is perhaps most similar to literature in its presentation of a sequence of events or situations to communicate its perception. When well done, with a valid comment, it is art; when not well done, or when it works to create emotional responses to shallow causes or people or situations, it is mass or pop culture that follows a "formula," providing an escape, and above all money for the maker. As in literature, we have to learn and teach the difference between quality and "kitsch."

The basic difference between film and literature is, of course, films *show* and literature *tells*. Both try to make the audience *see*, as George Bluestone wrote, "see visually through the eye or imaginatively through the mind. And between the percept of the visual image and the concept of the mental image lies the root difference between the two media." It is good to compare the two media. It is good to ask kids to convert one form to the other. It is good to use film as you would writing. The thought processes are the same — and, boy, will they spend more time on the film and involve many more skills and learnings than if they wrote an essay!

"Most teachers gravitate naturally toward a combination of the thematic and aesthetic approaches in what might best be termed 'a functional approach,' which strives to talk about the films in terms of total experience. Style is recognized not as something imposed on some pre-existing material but as the way in which the director conveys his inner meanings."

If you are leery or cautious, try one film a week or every two weeks. If films are hard to find in your district, use one of the supplement-to-literature films your school probably owns. Deal with the film; but try *not* referring to the book. Start, if you want to, doing what you would do with

Father John Culkin lists the possible approaches to film study in *his* pamphlet-book, **Film Study in the High School:**

Historical — the origin and growth of the motion pictures.

Sociological — the impact of film on society; film as propaganda; film as reflecting society: censorship; economics.

Comparative — the relation of film to the other arts.

Aesthetic — the relation of the material and formal elements of the medium.

Thematic — the analysis of the content and values of films.

Psychological — the effects of films on viewers.

Educational — the preparation and utilization of instructional films.

Creative — the production of films.

(Fordham Film Study Center, Bronx, N.Y., 1965), pp. 21–22.

the book. If you have, for example, the school release of *Huckleberry Finn*, starring Mickey Rooney, talk about the journey motif, the American con-artist myth, Huck's relationship to Jim, Huck as anti-hero, Tom Sawyer as some kind of norm, Twain's folk humor, as well as the characters and their development, the setting, and the surrounding history. Don't feel it is a waste of time to show the film more than once. Although film's outstanding characteristic is its immediacy, allow yourself and your class one of the luxuries of reading — being able to go back over parts for information, clarity, or pleasure. A natural outcome of this approach will be some attention to technique and form (how this part was filmed or how that scene was set up or appeared), and this should enrich the experience.

Please keep in mind that if every film you use in class is dealt with in the manner suggested above, you might soon encounter a film-avoidance reaction on the part of your students. I mention this approach more for your peace of mind than for students' love of and interest in film. I am, however, confident that this kind of attention, even to the scratched, cut version of *Huckleberry Finn*, will be profitable and will encourage you to delve more deeply into film study.

Too literary an approach, or too technical an approach, or too much emphasis on the development of the "motion picture" without attention to each person's experience, reaction, and emotional response to the film, is likely to place film study in the same category as *Silas Marner*. And if that happens, we have lost sight of the need to deal with films. We might, as Pauline Kael warns, "kill" the movies, or at least divorce the films viewed in school from life, and lose another chance to help our students understand that all imaginative work is related and that there are ways to deal intelligently with all such work from comic strips to *Satiricon*, from *Beowulf* to *Endgame*.

I believe that the best kind of film to use in school is the short, experiential-experimental film. These films fit into the school schedule, they are more easily obtained than feature films, they are cheaper, and they usually deal with one completely presented idea. They are more immediate — the topics are relevant and timely, and because they are timely, they are usually more avant-garde or experimental, and they can be dealt with for emotion, for expression, and as literature.

If you have access to a film library, read the catalogue carefully for such films, and order some for viewing. Find out if there is a county or city film library in your area that permits people to take out films in the way books are loaned. If there is, you have to pick them up and return them and are responsible for them, but these films are usually in much better condition than school films and well worth the trip to pick them up. Or, read magazines such as *Media and Methods*, or any school magazine, and order some films that are offered for previewing — maybe if your film study is successful your school will buy some of them.

The May 1970 issue of *Media and Methods* reported the results of a survey of 1,400 readers in response to many questions, one of which was

"List three most effective works used in the last few years" in several categories. I am including the short and feature-film responses.

Titles are listed according to the number of mentions they received. Year of release and distributor are given after each film.

1. An Occurrence at Owl Creek Bridge. 1962. (CON)

2. Why Man Creates. 1968. (PYR)

3. The Red Balloon. 1956. (BRA)

4. Night and Fog. 1955. (CON)

5. Phoebe. 1965. (CON)

6. Dream of Wild Horses. 1962. (CON)

7. Hangman. 1964. (CON)

8. Neighbors. 1952. (IFB)
   Stringbean. 1964. (CON)
   Parable. 1964. (PROT)

9. Moods of Surfing. 1968. (PYR)

10. Time Piece. 1966. (CON)

11. The Hat. 1965. (CON)
    Clay. 1964. (ACI)

Sixteen in Webster Groves. 1966. (CAR)
Toys. 1967. (CON)

12. The Hand. 1965. (CON)
    No Reason To Stay. 1966. (EBE)

13. Hunger in America. 1968. (CAR)

14. The Searching Eye. 1969. (PYR)
    The Golden Fish. 1962. (CHU)
    Harvest of Shame. 1960. (CON)

15. Run. 1962. (BRA)
    The War Game. 1966. (CON)
    The Critic. 1962. (BRA)

16. A Lover's Quarrel with the World. 1967. (HOLT)
    American Time Capsule. 1969. (PYR)
    Two Men and A Wardrobe. 1957. (CON)

17. Glass. 1958. (CON)
    Ski, the Outer Limits. 1969. (PYR)
    Black History — Lost, Stolen or Strayed. 1968. (BFA)

Conformity. 1964. (CAR)
The Adventures of an *. 1957. (CON)
Help, My Snowman's Burning Down. 1964. (CON)
You're No Good. 1966. (CON)
Nanook of the North. 1922. (CON)

18. Hemingway. 1961. (CON)
    A Time for Burning. 1966. (CON)
    A Chairy Tale. 1957. (IFB)

19. Very Nice, Very Nice. 1961. (CON)

The Game. 1967. (CON)

20. The Weapons of Gordon Parks. 1968. (CON)
    Eye of the Beholder. 1955. (SR)
    Leaf. 1962. (PYR)
    The Detached Americans. 1964. (CAR)
    Cities in Crisis. 1968. (UED)
    Chickamauga. 1963. (CON)
    Unicorn in the Garden. 1962. (BRA)
    Pigs. 1967. (CHU)

FEATURE FILMS

The top 20 feature films are a fascinating mix of films currently in (or very recently out of) theatrical release, and older films which have been touring the schools for some time. Keeping in mind that we asked readers to list the most effective feature films they have used with their kids over the past few years, we have concluded that the local movie house is serving as an important classroom resource. The big disadvantage here, of course, is that you cannot control programming. Add to this the two or three year lag between theatrical release and non-theatrical release, and the two or three additional years you have to wait till rental rates come down out of the ionosphere, and you have a lag of four to five years before feature films are really usable in the schools. One way out of this dilemma might be the CBS-EVR video playback system — advertised elsewhere in this issue.

Note that distributors are not listed for films still in theatrical release.

1. Romeo and Juliet. 1969

2. Easy Rider. 1969

3. Loneliness of the Long Distance Runner. 1962. (COS)

4. On the Waterfront. 1954. (GEN)

5. Nobody Waved Goodbye. 1964. (BRA)

6. Raisin in the Sun. 1961. (GEN)

7. David and Lisa. 1962. (COS)

8. To Kill A Mockingbird. 1962. (TWY, UNI)

9. Nothing But A Man. 1963. (BRA)

10. Lord of the Flies. 1963. (COS)

11. Citizen Kane. 1941. (FNC, BRA, AUD)

12. Midnight Cowboy. 1969

13. The Graduate. 1968

14. Grapes of Wrath. 1940. (BRA, COS, FNC)

15. Charly. 1968

16. La Strada. 1954. (BRA)

17. Billy Budd. 1962. (AUD)
    High Noon. 1952. (GEN)

18. High School. 1969. (OST)
    Ox Bow Incident. 1943. (BRA, FNC)

19. 2001: A Space Odyssey. 1968
    Death of a Salesman. 1951. (GEN)

20. Last Summer. 1969
    The Learning Tree. 1969

OK — let's say you get the films — what to do now? How to study films in a good way? Film study usually follows a view-them—respond-to-them—discuss-them pattern.

First of all, you should *never* show a film without previewing it. If you don't really respond to the film in some way during the previewing, consider not showing it. If you decide to show it but you are not interested in or enthusiastic about it, why not tell your students how you feel and see if a student would like to be in charge of doing something with that film — or maybe you should have a student do it without knowing how you feel — or maybe students should be in charge as much as you are, anyway. The important thing is that the films must be dealt with from real interest and enthusiasm; you can't fake that.

If a person maintains conviction that the basic complexity behind a film is just as important as the complexity behind a poem or a novel, he doesn't make the mistake of feeling that everyone understands a film just because he sees it. Of course, one of the major goals of film education is to help students see, but given the complexity of the material and the possible range of perceptions, responses, and interpretations, that goal is not a simple one, nor can it be the only one.

A set of guidelines for a film classroom:

1. Do not lecture before showing the film. Do not tell the students what to look for.

2. Show the film under the best possible conditions for viewing and hearing. Darken the room and put the speaker in front of the audience.

3. Have a short break after showing the film, if possible.

4. Discuss the picture — not ideas in general.

5. Give specific examples when you discuss.

6. As a moderator, be brief. Do not let a few students dominate the discussion.

7. Try to relate each remark to the remark of the previous speaker.

8. Indicate the way in which the camera conveys ideas.

9. The success of a discussion does not depend on whether students agree with the moderator or not.

10. After the class has seen several films together, the moderator should expect or suggest cross-references and comparisons among films.

11. After the discussion, comment on the way the discussion progressed, without giving answers to the film or the discussion. The ideas are important, not the number of "right answers."

DAVID SOHN

Wait. Let things happen. Listen to what your students say. Ask someone who has made films to come in to talk to your students. Compare TV shows and ads to the films you see. Work out what makes a good film. Spend time on animation and maybe ask them to make a flip series. Talk about what is said in one film compared to what is said in another. Write words or narration for silent films. Have your students keep a journal to record their responses to the films. Ask them to try to write what happened scene by scene, and play the film over again to see how closely they observe and remember. But please, don't overteach. And don't, despite what others might advocate, just show films and never discuss them (as happens with the TV and most movies the students see outside school), but find a middle ground that deals with the student's responses to a film that he shares and works out communally with the class.

There have been many books published in the last few years to help teachers study the short film. Most of the best are described in Chapter X. I would recommend the following: *Willowbrook Cinema Study Project*, by Ralph J. Amelio (George A. Pflaum, 1969), *Film Study in the High School*, by John Culkin (Fordham Univ. Film Study Center, Bronx, N.Y., 1965), and *Film Making in Schools* by Douglas Lowndes (Watson-Gutpill, 1970).

If you would like to try a film and literature study, keeping attention close to the literature method (after all, this is where our competency and training lie, so why not start with what you know and are most comfortable with and move from there?), perhaps the following could be used as guidelines.

First, like a novel, nearly every film has at least one theme, possibly more. In what way is the theme supported or developed through the plot? This can be tricky; films often rely more on plot than on theme for their statement and effectiveness, because kinetic media naturally emphasize motion and movement.

A comparative study of film and literature is often instinctive — how many times have you heard "The movie was better than the book" or the reverse? A natural beginning is to explore the changes that occur when a work of literature is transferred to another medium. For example, dramas are often filmed as stage events, maintaining the proscenium arch, but what happens when the camera leaves the theater seat and provides multiple views? As useful as this response is, it is also logically and esthetically unfair to both the printed and visual media; their limitations and opportunities are comparable — but different.

How are setting and mood established? Does the filmmaker have many devices available? What are they? For instance, what is the effect of the sound track — or the effect of visual experience without sound? Some other technical considerations are slow motion, distorted colors, and extreme camera angles.

The central technical devices is editing: the selection and arrangement of images not necessarily shot in chronological sequence. This is the creative core of many films. Some considerations here are the distance between the camera and what is seen, sudden cuts, juxtaposition of images, sequential interruptions, fades, or time-lapse photography. One of the most important and interesting considerations is the location of the camera eye — the viewpoint forced upon the viewer. How is the point of view given, and what effect does it have? What relationship does the point of view establish between the characters — and between the viewers and the image? How are the point-of-view techniques similar to those in literature?

What about symbolization and characterization? Do symbols have more impact when they can be seen? Are there different methods and problems of character development in film and literature? Which has more impact and possible meaning; does a smile, or the description of a smile, have more impact and meaning?

Another consideration is the relation of space and time to visual and printed media. Their problems need to be examined in the dual context of the creator and the audience. You can't put a movie down — you can watch faster than you can read. What are the differences, if any, in problems of "suspended disbelief"? Is the visual image more "real" than the written image?

To be more specific about what to discuss the staff of the "Film as Rhetoric" program at the University of Illinois has suggested the following general questions for studying the experimental film:

What is the filmmaker trying to say? Is there a theme or message to his work?

Is the title of the film an arbitrary label, or does it give some structure or meaning to the work?

Is the film effective? (I.e., does it persuade you or convince you of the validity of its point?) Why does it work?

What cinematic techniques does the filmmaker use and why? (E.g., why color, rather than black and white, or vice versa; why one kind of background music rather than another; why one photographic style rather than a different one?)

What general rhetorical techniques does the filmmaker use and why? (E.g., irony, juxtaposition, repetition, etc.)

What structure is evident in the film? (E.g., linear or cyclical, general to particular, static or progressive, etc.)

Tone: how does the filmmaker treat his audience?

Mood: how does the filmmaker treat his subject?

Emphasis: what object or objects does the camera choose to focus upon? To a certain extent, film is just as important for what it excludes as for what it includes. What is the filmmaker's criterion for his selection of details?

What assumptions about the sympathies and viewpoints of his audience does the filmmaker make? What kind of an audience is the film geared to?

What are the predominant visual images of the film? Which ones do you remember, and why? What visual qualities of the film most appealed to you?

So far we have been dealing with media as stimuli — responding ourselves, but focusing our attention on someone's imaginative response to his environment and how he worked it out. We carry on most of our relationship with media as absorbers — now how about considering using moving media as a vehicle for our own responses? It should heighten our perception of all the messages that are sent out to us; but also, and equally important, it should help us be comfortable with the surrounding technology, and provide us and our students with many more possibilities and means to express responses to our environments and to literature.

Students' private and unknown metaphors and visions may be better communicated through sound and visual expressions than through the written word. For them, writing and print have so many unpleasant connotations — maybe we owe it to them to open up other possibilities for response. How can we expect a student to respond fully if we keep him confined to the narrow path of writing? Especially when you consider how much of his life is not written down.

In order for the class (teacher and students) to respond in terms of moving media naturally, they must first feel comfortable or at least familiar with the forms — the machines and their materials and products.

It is safe to assume that almost everyone knows how to operate a record player, but how many people know that if the speakers of a record player are separate from the turntable, a tape recorder can be attached to the record player and kids can use the tape recorder's microphone as a loudspeaker system? Or am I getting ahead of myself?

Records   Here is a virtually untapped natural (for schools) resource. All schools own records of English and American literature. Why not keep them spread around in the English classrooms near a record player so students can listen to them whenever they want to? If your school does not have enough record players for every teacher to have one in his room, why not go out and buy a secondhand "high fidelity" record player yourself, and buy a new needle for it? And bring in records — or ask your students to. And if they want to hear rock music while they work, let them — they are used to doing things while music is on. Ask them to tell you or the class about what they bring in — what do they know about the group, the music, what the songs mean? — you'll be surprised about how much they know about the rock culture. Why not use what they know and love in school? Instead of, or along with, researching and reading a poet, why not a rock group with an analysis of their music? You will probably get exciting group discussions. Listen carefully. Look for places and things they are talking about that you can help expand, or things you can see might be continued for more class attention and time, or that needs some gaps to be filled.

Or why not study comedy, using records, or speeches, or dialects? Why not use the music from *West Side Story* as a setting for *Romeo and Juliet*? Talk about the subjects of American music from spirituals to Charles Ives, to jazz, to rock, to folk, to country and western, to pop; then listen to it. Compare American folk music with French or Irish folk music; or consider war songs or labor songs. You could take up anything that is on records in your classroom universe of discourse. A record store becomes a library of lesson-plan inspirations.

Tape recorders They are quite easy to operate in all their forms, and most schools have them. If your class has not used them much, why not try a verbal essay together as a class, and tape-record the procedure to play it back and then keep it around to refer to? The first thing many students may secretly be dying to do is to listen to their own voices on tape if they have never done so. This can be done in a private manner. Have the tape recorder in the room for several days and let the kids use it for ten or fifteen minutes apiece. When they are generally satisfied with that, turn them loose to act on an idea of their own. You could suggest taping interviews; or sounds made on the school bus; or people's comments on one subject, to create verbal collages; or sections of rock music that are concerned with the same theme — you can be sure the class won't have any difficulty working with theme in that context.

Or you could ask the students to make tape commercials to appeal to different social groups. They could use a real product or business or in-vent one. Ask them to do a tape script in three parts; what they say, what they mean, and what their intended audience thinks it hears. This could lead to anything — analysis of television, magazine, radio, and billboard advertising for methods of persuasion or for the uses of music or design. Or you could begin a propaganda study; or you could plan to effect a change in student government in the school — using advertising for politi-cal purposes, as is becoming more and more a part of political campaigns (and, some would say, created at least one of our recent presidents, as shown in *The Selling of the President*).

Instead of a film festival in your class, what about a tape festival? In groups of two or three, or by themselves, ask members of the class to enter a ten-minute tape to be judged and voted upon by the class at the festival. Anything that can be recorded qualifies. If they need suggestions, offer them, and if you see that some kids are working on a theme and you know a good poem or story that applies, offer it to them. Watch the stu-dents carefully to notice what things they are interested in, and store the information for later use. Make yourself a service person for them — if they need something and don't know how to get it, suggest a way for them to get it. Before the actual recording is done, maybe you could have a workshop set up, where each group tells the rest of the class its idea and asks for suggestions, and the class works out ways to do it together. The prize for the festival could be that the class will create an environment for the winning tape. In this way the class will support and respond to stu-dent-created material.

The other major form or moving medium that schools have been equipping themselves for is filmmaking. Film study most often leads to filmmaking, but it could result from something like a tape festival; or it could be generated out of a novel study, a poem, a condition in the school or community, another film — anything, really. Making a film is much more complicated than making a tape recording, because there are many more parts and steps and considerations and instructions involved. If you

THE BASIC VOCABULARY OF THE GRAMMATICAL STRUCTURE OF FILM

SHOT   that which takes place in front of the camera from the time the camera starts until it stops

SCENE   a series of related connected shots

SEQUENCE   a group of related scenes in a given time and location

The transition from one scene to another consists of

CUT   straight switch from one shot to another

FADE   gradual darking of the film to blackness, followed by the opening up of a new scene

DISSOLVE   the melting of the last scene of a sequence into the first of another

Edward Fischer explains how the camera is used in his book *The Screen Arts*:

The basic shot sequence is long shot, medium shot, close-up, and reestablishing shot.

The long shot, also known as an establishing shot, shows the main object in relation to its general surroundings. The medium shot shows the main object in relation to its immediate surroundings. A close-up includes only the main object and usually only the important part of it. The re-establishing shot reorients the audience as to what surrounds the main object. All of this might best be understood by looking at a simple sequence:

Long shot — The main street of a western town. At the far end of the street a man is riding in on horseback. He is leading a pack horse.

Medium shot — Man on horseback and pack horse continue along main street.

Close-up — Pack horse. A man is strapped across the saddle.

Re-establishing shot — The horseman continues along street and dismounts at sheriff's office.

If ten excellent cameramen were given this script each would shoot the scenes a little differently. Some of the long shots would be longer than others and some of the close-ups would be closer than others. The choice of high and low angles would vary. Each cameraman would put his stamp on his way of telling the story as Rouault and Cézanne put their stamps on their paintings.

Sometimes, for a good reason, the camera starts with a close-up, moves back to a medium shot and then moves back to a long shot. This is especially useful for shock effect. A close-up of a limp hand with a revolver beside it; a medium shot of a man sprawled on a shabby sofa; a long shot of the sofa in a gritty room. The reaction to this close-up is different from what it would have been had the camera started with a long shot and worked in to the limp hand with the revolver. The audience would have been more prepared for it this way.

have never made a film before, how can you go about it?

There is the school of thought that completely follows "learn by doing" and says, Give the kids a camera and a film can, let them read the instructions, load the camera, and start shooting. When they get their film back from the developer, they'll see what they've done and what to do with it and what's wrong with it and what to do next.

I believe this is probably true. The students will most likely see that they should have held the camera at a different angle in spots, or focused, or not panned so much — technique is probably best learned by viewing mistakes and analyzing them. But I also think that starting with a single, simple assignment and paying attention to how the equipment works and how to care for it might be better. Beginning school filmmaking usually uses 8mm silent film; 8mm is the cheapest to buy and have developed, and if families have cameras and projectors that they are willing to lend, they are usually 8mm. I would also advocate not attempting sound with your first films unless you have a very large budget, a lot of equipment, and someone who knows something about it.

For a start you could get some raw 16mm film (the size film-school projectors use) and scratch on it or draw on it with felt-tip pens. Or you could try and get old throw-away film from a television studio or a motion picture service establishment. Or you could write to a film distributor and ask, if not for film, for places to get old film. Ask your students to make a film just by cutting and splicing (editing) bits and pieces together. Then you could ask your students to make a one-minute film, and go on from there. The following steps are suggested for a film your students must think out, film, and edit.

1. Idea: what would you like to show?

2. Subject: what do you want to film to illustrate your idea — what is your "story"?

3. Shots: what specific scenes or things do you want to film?

4. Sequence: what order do you want them to be in?

5. Storyboard or shot script: all the preceding steps should lead to some kind of script — a two-column layout, one column detailing what you want to film and exactly why you want to film it, and the other stating the significance or order of the sequence in relation to the film.

6. Film: go out with a camera and film and all the necessary props and actors and equipment and light, and begin filming.

7. Development of the film: most school filmmakers send the film out to be developed. Ask the shop you choose for a school discount and tax exemption. Also check around for wholesale services (and film).

8. Viewing: when the film comes back from the developer, view it many times, note what is good and bad. Discuss. Decide what, if anything, needs to be reshot, and reshoot.

9. Editing: for this you need a film editor, a splicer, and film-splicing tape. The best thing to do is take a stick shaped like a yardstick and put small nails or pins in it at half-inch intervals. Nail this onto another stick to form a *T*. Using the second stick as a base, stand the *T* in a grocery-store-size box. Put all the film you want to use on the nails in final sequence as you cut them. Put the throw-away film in the box.

10. Splice the good or saved pieces together.

11. View the finished product.

12. Decide if you want to make a tape to go with the film or leave it silent.

13. Show the film.

A wonderful source for film study is comic strips. Comic strip's technique is similar to film's; they contain cuts and movements and dialogue and continuity and closeups. You could ask your students to bring in a comic book or the comic strip page from the newspaper and mark each frame for camera technique — the more they learn about film the more complex these marks will become. You could bring in one of the numerous paperback film scripts or screen plays that have appeared recently and compare the camera moves and cuts, etc., to the ones the students suggested for the comics.

The students could try drawing their own cartoons and marking them. They could make flip books by drawing a figure or object on the corner of a book page with slightly different movements on each page and then flipping the book with their thumbs and watching the figure move. This is the clearest way to explain how film actually works. The film goes past the projector at 24 frames per second but the human eye retains what it last saw for one tenth of a second. Together these two factors fool the brain into thinking it sees a *moving* picture.

One kind of film uses many still pictures on the same subject or theme. Lay out the pictures and shoot, keeping them on the camera long enough for the purpose of the film. The briefest amount of time is about two frames.

Another idea might be a careful, close study of a painting. Perhaps your class would like to do a film that tells the story depicted in a painting or a photograph or several paintings or photographs using close-ups and other methods of detailed attention by moving the camera. They could make a tape narration to go along with it.

Once the various forms of media have been mastered to some degree,

Judge Parker

3 Frames or 3 Scenes or 1 Sequence

1
Establishing shot
Tight framed
Action in foreground

2
Medium shot
Action in foreground
No background
Action to left

3
Reverse angle
Eye moves from foreground
to background
Action to right
Great depth of field
Foreground static
Motion in background

why shouldn't the students work in a multi-media fashion — using ideas or themes and creating their own responses out of many choices. Active choices — making things, and passive choices (which includes private responses and reactions), such as viewing, observing, reading things. Or why not a class settling on love or war or mass hysteria or *Hamlet* or poetry as the primary focus or unifying theme? Let them decide how and in what combinations to passively and actively participate. Passive to active participation would include reading and then writing; viewing films, photographs, poetry, and then creating films, photographs, and poetry. All media — tapes, slides, photographs, painting, design, graphics, speech, records, mime, acting — become areas for response because all communicate. All can be studied and all are possible as means for student expression. If you begin to think about your classroom as part of the universe of discourse, multi-media becomes the natural answer.

The study of film when integrated with the study of literature allows the students to see how each medium works and to explore the similarities and differences between the two media. When students study film and literature together, they are able to understand not only the meaning or message of a particular work of art, but also what each medium is forced to do, what it is able to do most successfully, and what it seems unable to do.

JOHN KATZ

Well then . . . media is to be taken in and loved and responded to. Film is someone's response, just as is a poem or a story. So there it is — someone's response and something to respond to. We could ask our students to write a poem on the same subject as the film they just saw. We should pay attention to why some things do better in one form than another and pay attention to the transformations that are necessary with each form change. We might get a sense of what filmic vision is, or glory of glories, we might even acquire a little visual literacy.

A response centered curriculum that cultivates understanding of communications media as part of all of life seems like a good philosophy and method to approach the universe of discourse with.

Students' and teachers' school lives would be so much richer if we could integrate what goes on outside school with what goes on inside — inside our school and inside ourselves. School is an institution that brings us together — well, why not *be* together when we are in school then?

RESPONDING
THROUGH VISUAL
SYMBOLS

It may or may not be true that a picture is worth a thousand words, but there certainly are pictures that can evoke a thousand words from some people at some time. Here's one:

If all the words that have been spoken or written about the *Mona Lisa* were strung end to end, they would reach considerably beyond the end of Pinocchio's nose. And an analysis of those words would show that certain words are used again and again in response to it: *beauty, serenity, enigmatic smile, composure*. Over the years the *Mona Lisa* has achieved the reputation of symbolizing those things.

And that's a marvelous quality of pictures: they can become a short-hand for expressing feelings, ideas, moods, and points of view. That quality derives from our private and collective experiences with certain objects, colors, and designs.

What feeling idea, mood, or point of view do these pictures call to your mind?

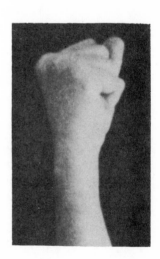

A hundred other people responding to the same pictures would undoubtedly make many of the same associations you did. The reason for that is so simple it hardly needs to be stated: pictures have symbolic value. To the extent that we share culture, that value is common; to the extent that each of us combines different cultural experiences, that value is unique.

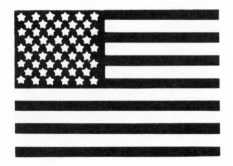

What does all of that have to do with teaching English?

The study of English is, as much as anything else, the study of symbolic actions. Making and using words is one form of symbolic action; making and using gestures is another; and making and using pictures is still another. And there are many more.

In a program geared to promote student response to literature, we want to encourage as many modes of symbolic action as possible. Responding with words — even in the English class — may or may not be any better than responding by

  (1) selecting a picture,
  (2) drawing or painting a picture,

                                                                or

  (3) making a collage or montage

that represents a mood, idea, feeling, or association that a particular experience with literature arouses.

The only test is

An honest response is what we are after, and an honest response shouldn't have to be defended. But it can be studied, discussed, and compared with other honest responses in an effort to arrive at fuller communication and greater self-insight.

> *Caution: Forcing students to defend honest responses can cause them to make dishonest ones.*

For instance:

Teacher.   What did you think of Sara Teasdale's "Barter," Mary?
Mary: I thought it was beautiful. Life really does have loveliness to sell.
Teacher: Very good, Mary. How about you, John?
John: I thought it was dumb and sickeningly sweet.
Teacher: In what way?
John: Well, it's just so sentimental.
Teacher: What particular things in the poem struck you as being sentimental?
John: Well, the whole idea that if you'll work hard, you'll be rewarded for it.
Teacher: Don't you agree with that, John?

and on . . .
and on . . .
and on . . .

Note that John, who dared to be honest, and who was no less articulate than Mary initially, had to go on to defend, defend, and defend his response. But Mary, that good little girl who said what the teacher wanted to hear, was praised and let off the hook. The next time John is asked a question by that teacher, he will, if he is smart, say what he knows the teacher wants to hear.

THAT'S THE WAY THE GAME IS PLAYED.

BARTER

Life has loveliness to sell —
All beautiful and splendid things,
Blue waves whitened on a cliff,
Climbing fire that sways and sings,
And children's faces looking up,
Holding wonder like a cup.

Life has loveliness to sell —
Music like a curve of gold,
Scent of pine trees in the rain,
Eyes that love you, arms that hold,
And, for your spirit's still delight,
Holy thoughts that star the night.

Spend all you have for loveliness;
Buy it and never count the cost.
For one white, singing hour of peace
Count many a year of strife well lost,
And for a breath of ecstasy
Give all you have been or could be.

SARA TEASDALE

But suppose the teacher had said, "I'd like each of you to read Teasdale's poem, "Barter," tonight and select an object or picture that suggests or represents your response to it." The result might have been that

Mary brought in this picture:

John brought in this series of pictures:

Jane brought in:

Bill brought in:

The teacher could then ask, "What is there about this poem or about us that could evoke so many different responses?" A lot of discussion could ensue, and nobody need be on the defensive hook.

Or suppose that the teacher hadn't specified the mode of response, and the result was this:

Mary wrote a poem.

John brought in a collage.

Jane did a pantomime.

Bill brought in a poster.

Sue wrote an essay.

Jim brought in a record.

All the better! The teacher could ask the same question as before, plus this one: "What dictated the mode of expression you chose: something about the poem, something about you, or something about what you wanted to say?"

It can work either way

It can also work the other way, that is, with the teacher choosing the pictures and letting the students select the one that is closest to their impressions, understandings, or total responses. After having students read "The Most Dangerous Game," the teacher could present the students with these three pictures:

Then the teacher could ask, "Which of these men most closely resembles what you think General Zaroff should look like?" A discussion of the responses could lead students to clarify their responses to the character, to come face to face with their stereotypes, and to test their understandings against others.

Or the teacher might bring in many different pictures of men with different expressions on their faces and ask the students to select the appropriate expressions for the various characters at different points in the story.

Or if the class were studying *A Separate Peace*, the teacher might bring in posters like:

The question, of course:
Which poster would Phineas choose for his room, and which would Gene choose?

All of these sorts activities, with the teacher selecting the visuals to bring into class would

a   provoke discussion

b   promote response

c   provide evidence of understanding

Using the same ideas, the students could individually or in groups present visuals to the class, asking

which of these scenes best fits the mood of the poem?

which colors best suit the personalities of the characters?

which of these objects would this poet or character most like to own?

which scene would this writer be most apt to write about?

which collage comes closest to your total response to the poem?

The beauty of such activities is that they promote involvement; stimulate response; require understanding, interpretation, synthesis, and evaluation; translate the vague and abstract into concrete images; provide a basis for comparing and contrasting ideas; force commitment; and

MAKE THE CLASS INTERESTING

Take collages, for example

Collage-construction makes for an excellent creative exercise in which individual students or groups of students might attempt to express an artistic assimilation of world/life/reality . . .

Normally a collage is of a photographic nature (i.e. pictures assembled from other pictures), but it need not be so restrictive. All sorts of materials have served many a sculptor or painter (Picasso made a snorting Taurus from the more mundane construct of bicycle seat and handlebars), and glass fragments, bottlecaps, peanut butter, coat hangers, sea shells, buttons, beads, etc. have all had their place in artistic expressions. What we are concerned with here is the picture collage, however, other materials should be kept in mind and can be introduced at any effective point in the construction of the collage.

The problem the student faces is that of any kind of composition. There are some necessary steps. Choosing the subject. Narrowing the topic. Gathering the material. Arranging the material. If there is a stack of old picture magazines around, finding the material is not hard. The student must however decide what the collage is to deal with; love for example, and then decide whether it is to be romantic love or love of all kinds. A tone must be chosen too — cynical? romantic? objective?

In making a collage the student should consider various questions about arrangement and organization:

a) Is he more interested in having the viewers see each integer-component (picture) or more interested in the viewer's deriving an over-all impression of the total collage?

b) Is he intending to create an impression of unity or of diversity?

c) Is he intending to use only photos, or will he consider other materials such as wire, string, bottlecaps, shells, etc.?

d) Is he intending the collage to be entirely non-verbal?

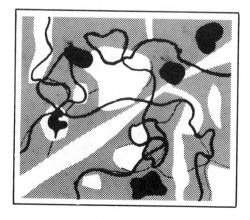

To have the viewer come away *with a general impression, the collage-maker should place the small parts close to each other.*

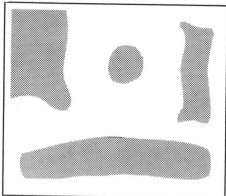

To have *the reader come away with a sense of parts, the collage-maker should make the parts distinctive by increasing the size of the individual components or by increasing space between components.*

Having made that first decision, the collage maker should pick his subject, and select and cut the pieces that he wants to use.

Next, in arranging the parts, the collage-maker should *not* think like a writer—that is, in terms of moving from left to right and from top to bottom—but like an artist, in terms of the whole visual space on whatever surface he is using. He should block that space into some large pattern like one of those on the facing page.

The shaded portions represent those parts of the collage that would contrast in such characteristics as color, lightness, type or clarity of picture. Each pattern leads the eye in a different way — into the center of the space, or away from it in a sweep; in a progression; to a sense of balance or precariousness.

The students might experiment with various patterns — placing the pictures or other materials in several patterns until they have achieved a pattern that they find suits their ends in making the collage. Once they have chosen the pattern, they can proceed to affixing the materials to the sheet.

There is no need to make the collage on a rectangular flat surface: successful collages have been applied to beach balls, made in a triangular form, applied to cutout figures, applied to the insides of boxes with peep-holes cut in various places on the sides. Each of these forms of the collage creates a special effect, one which uses the total space symbolically.

If the students decide that they are less concerned with the total impression than with individual parts, they are creating a picture essay. In this case, the layout of the pictures and the words should be such that there is some background space around each picture, separating the parts from each other. Despite this difference from the collage, the picture essay should be so arranged on the total space as to make a pattern that will lead the eye from picture to picture in the sequence that the creator wants.

An alternative to the picture collage is the sound collage. Suppose, for example, that students choose to make a sound collage about the school. The best way for them to do so would be to use two tape record-ers. With the first one, students would go around the school for several days, gathering such typical sounds as — noises of classes, class changes, lunch periods, guidance interviews, the custodians cleaning the building, sports events. Then they would play these random sounds onto a second tape, putting sounds together or taping one sound over another, in any order they find effective.

After students have made their picture collages and/or sound col-lages, let them present their work to the rest of the class. The class might well comment on or discuss the effect of the finished products.

One task students like to undertake is the illustrated anthology. There are many models in the recent high-school anthologies like those edited by Stephen Dunning and Geoffrey Summerfield (see Chapter X).

Begin by asking students to assemble their favorite poems or stories. They can reproduce them from current texts or anthologies. They can then choose the pictures that might go with the selections, and the order in which pictures and selections might be placed.

Should the anthology maintain a single focus, a single mood?

Should the pictures support the selections, or should they undermine them?

Should the pictures break up the text? Should the text be printed over the pictures so the pictures show through?

Should the text be single column or double column?

What kinds of type faces should be used?

Should there be little marginal quotations, like the marginal drawings in MAD?

Should the pictures be entirely black and white? Color? Mixed?

Should there be any section titles?

Should there be any introduction? Does the anthology explain itself?

What if the student wanted to introduce line drawings? Should they be mixed with photographs or with reproductions of paintings or statues?

These are but a few of the questions people need to answer in making a book of any sort. When your students make their anthologies, they have to deal with all the questions professionals tackle. Not that you would expect their work to be professional. But doing a project can help a person understand what has gone into something he might ordinarily take for granted. Perhaps your students will look at their anthologies more critically. That wouldn't hurt.

It doesn't always have to be collage or anthologies. Encourage students to

make centerfolds for novels   make maps

make cartoons

make response charts   make transparencies

make caricatures

make book jackets   make posters

make illustrations

which represent all or part of their responses to all or part of the literary experiences they have had, are having, or will have.

Some students, with some literature, cannot make an immediate verbal response to the experience, but they might be able to respond graphically. Different experiences elicit or demand different modes of response or symbolic action from different people.

Q. *Does all of this mean that an English teacher has to be an art teacher?*

A. Absolutely not. Primitive art has charm. Don't fuss about technique, just the statement that's being made.

Q. *How do I begin?*

A. Graphically.

Q. *What does that mean?*

A. Illustrate your own graphic response to give the kids an idea of what you mean.

Q. *What would represent "one small step for mankind"?*

A. Ask students to associate their favorite book, movie, poem, or play with a color.

Q. *Then what?*

A. Think about it, then talk about the associations.

Q. *What materials do I need to begin?*

A. Magazines, scissors, paste, glue, crayons, paper, transparencies, grease pencils, and anything else you can requisition. But not all of the work has to be done in class; it can be done at home as well. There the kids can worry about getting their own materials.

Q. *How should I evaluate graphic responses?*

A. On the basis of the amount of effort a student has put forth to make an honest representation of a sincere response. I would rather not grade them, but if I had to, that would be the basis.

Q. *As an English teacher, shouldn't I be more interested in promoting verbal responses?*

A. Probably yes, but it has been quite well established that each person has a preferred sense for taking in and storing stimuli, and it is probably true that each person also has a preferred medium for expressing responses to various stimuli. For those whose preference is verbal, beginning with a graphic response might be the best avenue for arriving at a verbal response.

Q. *Any guarantees?*

A. Nope.

DRAMA IN
THE ENGLISH CLASS

You'd like your tenth-graders to read Ferenc Santa's "Nazis," let us say. An exquisite little horror story, without violence, almost without incident. But it has caught you, because in the story Santa has distilled the very essences of totalitarianism, of rule by force. You realize that much of the impact the story has on you is due to the knowledge and experiences and memories you bring to its reading. Your students lack these things. What you want is for your students to respond viscerally to "Nazis." You know that most of them have not been prepared by life to so respond, and that talk and discussion and analysis will not produce the sort of intuitive apprehension of totalitarianism that "Nazis" can give the reader who is ready for it.

But, perhaps, if you can contrive to give the students a version of the experiences of the characters in the story, maybe then they will understand. It is worth a try. Take this scene, during the entire course of which the child's grandfather continues to chop wood, pretending to ignore what is going on.

The armed one leaned his boot against the child's side.

"Turn around!"

There, farther off, was the flock, grazing, without a single bell, not a single bell around the neck of one of them.

"Call the dog."

The boy called the dog. It sidled over slowly, then slunk up to the youngster and sat down at his feet.

"Pay attention!" said the armed one. "This thing lying at your feet, what is it?"

"A dog," said the child.

"No . . . This thing lying at your feet is a goat, a big white goat! Do you understand me?"

The boy was silent.

The armed one put the truncheon on the boy's uncovered head. He laid it across it, neatly bisecting the convexity of the skull so that the end of the stick protruded well ahead of the boy's eyes. The other armed one came nearer, halted his horse alongside the boy, close by, so close that the shank of the man's boot was tight against the boy's shoulder.

"Well?"

The child looked at the dog.

The armed one who had just came up to the child took his rubber stick and lightly placed it on the boy's shoulder.

"Say it nicely . . ."

"Well? . . . What's this thing in front of you?"

"A goat . . ." he said.

"A big white goat!"

"A big white goat."

Hannah Arendt said that the most horrifying thing about Eichmann was his ordinariness. Ferenc's insight is that the horrifying thing about the Nazis is their childishness. The armed ones are simply playground bullies with unlimited power, free to indulge themselves. Their victims cannot fight back, protest, or appeal for justice. Two armed men on horses against an old man and a child.

Act it out: establish the physical relationships

the utter helplessness of the two civilians

the gratuitous cruelty of the armed men

the child's fear and incomprehension

the old man's fear and outrage and frustration which he dare not express.

To prepare the students

Have them scream silently, putting the muscles of their entire bodies into it, but not making a sound. Then finally have them release the screams. Do it again, not releasing the tension. Tell them to feel the scream in their throats, their stomachs, their shoulders, their chests, and legs.

Then have them put the heel of a hand under their chins and push back till it hurts (as the Nazis do to the old man in another scene). Have them concentrate on maintaining a serene expression while holding this position; then ask them to smile. Push harder, smile broader.

(Interestingly, one cannot, in this position, say, "Free man"; but he can quite easily say, "Slave." Might be a point there to be made.)

Have them close their eyes and imagine the worst pain they can conceive of, really feel it, feel their muscles contract and writhe as the pain becomes unbearable. Let them feel the pain and react to it with all their bodies. Except for their faces — the facial expression must be kept neutral, unexpressive.

Then get volunteers to dramatize the scene. Line up some chairs, upon the seats of which the armed men will walk as the scene is played, always keeping their positions above the old man and the boy. Let one student read the narrative portions, the others moving as dictated and speaking in character. If the students have trouble with the dialogue, read it yourself the first time, as they mime the scene. Or read the story to them to establish the sequence of events, and let them improvise the dialogue.

Concentrate on the physical relationships and the physical contacts — the pressings and shovings. Try it in slow motion. Concentrate on what the old man feels as the boy is abused. Go through the scene once. Exchange parts, the oppressors becoming the victims. Do it again. Then stop and have the students sit down and relax.

Talk with them about their experiences with bullies. Ask them how they have felt when they have been forced by a bigger child or a parent or a teacher to say something they did not feel or something they knew was untrue. Ask them if they have ever bullied a younger child or taken advantage of someone else's weakness or ignorance. Ask them why they did it and how they felt when they were doing it.

Have them stop and imagine themselves in a position of absolute power over another. How would they act?

Have each student take an object — a large plastic bag, an empty cardboard box. It represents an enemy, something evil. Have them close their eyes and work themselves into a rage at whomever or whatever the object represents. Then, as they feel it, have them destroy the objects. But at leisure, smiling all the while, concentrating on their sensations as they smash and tear the objects.

Then back to "Nazis," with different actors. Enact the scene, concentrating on the feelings both expressed and unexpressed, and the ways they flow out of the physical relationships of the actors. Have four more students do the scene, then four more. Give everyone a chance.

Then stop and let the students talk about it. Or just think about it, if they wish.

Then do something else. You've taught "Nazis."

One reason for using drama: It enables you to accomplish things you cannot accomplish in any other way.

There are other reasons, involving the claim that drama provides some effective ways of doing things we now do in other ways, but not especially well and not with all students. But let us stick to the specific and get to the general later.

Even if there were not all sorts of good pedagogical and humanitarian reasons for using drama, English teachers would eventually be forced into it simply because so many of our contemporary poets are writing poems explicitly intended for performance.

> Surely there has never been a culture in
> which good poets were paid so well or
> played so important a part in the lives of so
> many young people as they do in ours,
> today. But teachers still, many of them,
> introduce students to poetry as if it were
> news. And you can still hear echoes of the
> elitist lament that there is no audience
> for poetry in a democratic mass culture.

If we could overcome our professional prejudices against the new and the popular and the public, if we were really interested in eliciting responses rather than conveying information, we should be hard put to justify giving, say, William Cullen Bryant a place in the curriculum over Bob Dylan or John Lennon. But the delicacy of older (over 25) ears and the idea that listening to music is not a proper educational activity has left much of the best modern verse either beyond the pale or in the hands of the youth cultists in education.

There is, at any rate, a middle ground between close reading and public performance that is well worth a teacher's exploring. Here are a couple of verses from Joe McDonald's "Harlem Song," a neat and conventionally literary set of satirical lyrics:

Glorious . . . breathtaking . . . spectacular!
Relax in the grandeur of America's yesteryear
Harlem — the land of enchanting contrasts,
Where the romantic past touches hands
With the exciting present
First, the pleasure of being received
With warmth and genuine hospitality
Then, the easy adjustment to the comfort and style
Of superb meals, exotic beverages, colorful entertainment
And dynamite action
Doing all the wonderful things
That wonderful vacations are made of
At wonderful savings, too.
Yes, come to Harlem
The happy meeting ground for families with large wants
And small budgets . . .

Discover glorious Harlem in New York City
There's thrills and chills in the land of rhythm and blues
Bring the family to Harlem in New York City
They'll have fun in the sun doin' what the black folks do
And every little pickaninny
Wears a great big grin
Just hanging round and waiting
For some white folks to drop in
But if you can't go to Harlem — that's New York City
Maybe you'll be lucky and Harlem will come to you . . .

Imagine what you could do in the classroom with this poem, using the usual sorts of analysis and discussion. Then listen to what Country Joe and the Fish do with it. See whether you don't have to admit that their performance — with the movie-travelogue voice, the singer with the Rudy Vallee megaphone, the Hawaiian guitars, the final rifle shot — does not do a better job of illuminating the satirical points of the poem than all the "teaching" in the world could do. Then try turning over the lyrics of "Harlem Song" to your students to work out *their own* presentation of it, telling them to make it different from the record; make it theirs.

In the course of wrestling with the problems of presentation — voice, tone, pacing, effects, and so on — they will necessarily be engaging in just the sorts of meaningful analysis that they normally only watch the teacher engage in. And they will be enjoying it.

But not only rock lyrics. Most any recent printed collection of poems contains at least a few poems intended for performance — usually group or multimedia performance, and therefore ideal for the classroom. Jackson MacLow's "New Signals Hint at Neutron Stars," to take one elaborate example, consists of nine pages resembling the following:

NEUTRON STARS

Team
Picks
Up
Weak
Space
Impulses

new kind of
radio source have been dis- [sssssssssssssssssssssssssss]
covered by the
Mullard
Radio
Astronomy
Observatory at
Cambridge
University

The accompanying performance suggestions call for the poem to be reproduced and the pages distributed among any number of readers, several pages per reader. "Observe blank spaces after words in each line ... & between strophes," the notes tell us, "as silences equal in minimum length to words that might be printed in them.... Repeated letters are interpreted as final phonemes with minimal duration" equal to words that might be printed in the space.

One reader can read the entire poem as a solo while the other readers read those pages they have been given.

Readers may prolong silences & prolonged phonemes beyond durations indicated by space lengths following words. They must LISTEN. Each reader is to add new words to the total situation ... when it seems really best to do so. Each person's performance is to be modified by closely attending to the total sound, & each modifies the total sound by closely attending to his own.

Even so well-established an academic poet as James Schevil offers us "sound poems" like the following in his latest collection:

Woe ...
Woeoooh
Woeoooohh
Woehooo
Woooo
Wooohmb
Woooooommmmmb
... ahhh
Aaaaahh
Maaaah
Woee-maaaaah
Woeoo-maaaan

Woe-man
Wooh-**man**
Whoa-man
Whoa-man
Woe-**man**
Woe-man
Wo-**man**!

Try *that* on your new criticism!
Better yet, try it with your students.

The prosodic principles of Ron Penoyer's "Countdown" can be divined only in performance:

T minus 60 seconds
and counting
marbles on 4th Street
which Joey collected
since age 5-1/2
years ago the
buildings were new
but now they're
falling down
to T minus 50
on the Cape
and all systems are go
up the street
to Stuyvesant which
is the end of the
world and beyond
it are monsters breathing

jet propulsion fuel
now disconnected from
the pad at T minus 40
all systems are green
light at the corner
by the delicatessen
where meat is grown
in white wax paper
and milk is made in
bottles like the ones
Daddy brings home to the
pad now cleared at
T minus 30 while voice
communications with
the world through the
welfare worker are not
proceeding at T minus
20 and now removed
from the launching room
are 2 dead rats and
Mammy is screaming
10, 9, 8, 7 days till
the next check comes for
6, 5, 4, 3 dollars or even
2, 1, zero, ignition, Lift-off
to buy a pair of brand
new shining rockets

There are several voices at work here — the ground controller's and at least two others' whose comments are at different levels of generality. The word or words that end the contribution of one voice also begin the contribution of the next voice, and probably should be spoken by both voices, overlapping but not quite in unison. Let two or three or more students work together to locate these dual-purpose words and phrases as well as they can, and try reading the poem aloud, inventing appropriate deliveries for the various voices. (Toward the end, things get complicated and will have to be worked out in practice.)

When the readers have done the poem two or three times and seem to have it, ask another student to count down from 60, in a normal tone of voice at a normal speed, as the other students read the poem once again.

It will be discovered that the student counting down will be getting to 50, 40, 30, 20, just as the other readers do — the simple count serving the same purpose as the count of syllables and accents in more familiar poems. After 20, the verse runs ahead of the count, which, once the principle has been noted, suggests that the readers should slow down to stay with the counter or make other adjustments such as full repetitions of overlapping phrases. Try this one out and tape-record it. Let your students try writing this sort of poem. Perform their works.

Even more than the poets, contemporary playwrights demand performance. Many recent plays, especially those that were "written" improvisationally, really exist only in performance and simply cannot be read and studied as more verbal, conventional plays can be. The script of a play like Roland Van Zandt's excellent (but, I believe, still unpublished) *Woodrow Wilson in the Promise Land* rather resembles notes on an evening's TV entertainment, made by a stenographer in a TV showroom with all the sets going and tuned to different channels. The coherence and the unity of such a play are both discovered and created in its performance.

But, really, the difference between these contemporary plays and Shakespeare's is only one of degree. Playwrights (as distinct from poets and novelists writing in the dramatic mode) have always written for the actor rather than for the general reader. The main difference between *Lear* and the notes-upon-which-to-improvise in the latest drama magazine is that Shakespeare was probably the more gifted and more intelligent playwright. He wasn't doing anything different in kind from the modern author.

In teaching plays, therefore, drama is not just useful, it is clearly demanded. Every textbook introduction to a play says somewhere that the reader has to "visualize" a production of the play. But one has to do drama before one can imagine drama being done.

How does a child learn to "see things which are not really there? . . . The child who sees the objects and events described by a storyteller does so only because he has been exposed to complex contingencies involving actual events. . . . So far as we know, nothing is ever seen covertly which has not already been seen at least in fragmentary form.

B. F. SKINNER

To go at it another way, the playwright expects his readers — the actors and directors — to possess certain reading skills, certain imaginative capabilities, which they will have developed in the course of their experiences with drama. Therefore, he does not bother saying a great many things he intends, for he can count on his readers to re-create his intentions adequately.

One wouldn't open an essay addressed to professors of American literature with a sentence beginning, "Edgar A. Poe, the famous short-story writer and poet. . . ."

Neither did Shakespeare need to gloss Bernardo's "Who's there?" that opens *Hamlet* with a direction something like: *Nervously, coming to guard with his weapon; entertaining the possibility someone or some thing other than his friend may be on the platform, Bernardo irregularly issues the challenge to the sentry.*

If this reasoning is sound, it is disingenuous to expect a student adequately to respond to a printed play until he has been given a wide variety of experiences with drama — experiences that range from watching plays and creating them to acting from a script.

Even with students who have reached the stage where they can deal competently with printed plays, improvisations and mime and readings and the staging of scenes can be perhaps the most fruitful sort of critical activity, since fullness of comprehension and appreciation of qualities and nuances must precede effective interpretation. The same, of course, is true with nondramatic oral literature.

Drama can, as already shown, contribute to the teaching of shorter prose fiction and to the teaching of nonfiction prose that makes use of the narrative devices of the fictionist. Hanson Baldwin's classic account of the sinking of the *Titanic* comes to mind as a candidate for dramatic presentation, perhaps with the aid of slides, music, sound effects, and light-show effects.

Drama is perhaps of less direct usefulness with a whole novel, except in the form of free discussion of responses or the re-creation of key scenes. The sheer bulk of the novel insulates it from dramatic, as from formalistic, approaches.

Improvisation can, of course, be used to explore themes, confrontations, and characters, and to isolate and identify issues. Appropriate scenes or selections from a novel may be worked with dramatically or presented orally. Modern novelists who strive to show rather than to tell are especially suitable for dramatic adaptation and mime. But it will come as no surprise to teachers that even the best novelistic dialogue often is quite unsatisfactory when read aloud.

Drama is no cure-all. Drama all the time is as boring as anything else all the time. So far as our objective is to produce students who will read books when they are no longer students, drama is a means to the end of giving students pleasant and satisfying experiences with books.

Do you realize you've gotten all this way without a DEFINITION of *drama?*

Have you missed it?

Probably not any more than your students would miss your definitions of *simile, metaphor, symbol, motive,* and the like.

But, just in case, here is a definition:

**DRAMA IS ALMOST ANYTHING THAT GET KIDS UP OFF THEIR
PASSIVE FANNIES AND ENGAGES THEM ACTIVELY IN WORKING
OUT WAYS TO EXPRESS THEIR OWN FEELINGS, RESPONSES, PERCEPTIONS,
ATTITUDES, AND IDEAS.**

To put it another way, drama is a collection of devices for giving the students the chance to do the finding, structuring, organizing, selecting, and evaluating that textbook authors and teachers traditionally have tried to do for them.

Why be exclusive?

> Drama is a warm puppy.

And it is mime and improvisation and theater games and
movement and spontaneous, unstructured talk and dramatic
reading and choral reading and role-playing and play-making
and dramatizing stories and script-writing and singing and
rehearsing to act and acting from scripts and (within limits)
acting for an audience.

And almost anything else the reader wishes to include (are "simulation games" drama?), except sitting and absorbing information or doing what the boss tells you to do whether you want to or not.

A great deal of eloquent and reasoned discourse has lately been devoted to the promotion of drama in the English classroom. Much of the best of this literature has been sponsored or distributed by the National Council of Teachers of English; and with the writings of Geoffrey Summerfield, Gabriel Barnfield, James Moffett, Douglas Barnes, and the rest so easily and cheaply available, there is no point in spending a lot of space summarizing the case that has been made for drama. For the reader who is not yet familiar with the arguments made for drama, the following extended quotation from Douglas Barnes's excellent *Drama in the English Classroom* will serve as an adequate introduction.

In our increasingly industrial and urban societies, we need citizens who can give themselves warmly across the gulfs that divide man from man, and who can deal with the variousness and self-contradiction within themselves. This is one kind of communication without which society cannot survive. Schools can take only part of the responsibility for developing this kind of communication; insofar as they do, however, it will not be through imposing uniformity but through providing activities tending towards what we have called drama.

What we are recommending, even at college and university level, is an approach to all education that can reasonably be called "dramatic" in that it deals in complexes of attitudes rather than in simple certainties. It is through dramatic activity that we can most readily express, recognise, come to terms with, and begin to evaluate that variousness in others and in ourselves that is at once the wealth of humanity and the force that threatens to destroy it.

It will be clear to the reader that we have been using the word drama in a very inclusive way. . . . More than a series of activities to be followed in the classroom, we have implied an attitude towards the whole of education.

Arthur Eastman, identifying drama as basic to all literary forms, illuminates its power by emphasising its scope and depth:

"Drama is larger than literary — and earlier. It is mime and talk as well as script. It opens to the inarticulate and illiterate that engagement with experience on which literature rests. It permits them, and people in general, to discover their private human potentialities, to participate in and share the experience of the group, to make experience public.

". . . Drama is the . . . primal ocean in which the other literary forms float — monologue and dialogue, exposition, narration, description, argument, lyric, oration, epigram, apothegm. Drama is the source from which . . . other literary forms flow. . . .

"Drama liberates. It releases its practitioners from the inhibitions of self-consciousness. As it is play, make-believe rather than believe, it permits the individual to try on an attitude or to model an emotion without paying actuality's price.

It releases its practitioners, too, from the explicit interpretive restraints more common in other forms of literature. The actor may and must find within himself what it is to be jealous, envious, distraught, ambitious. Finally, as the practitioner becomes creator, drama opens to him the discovery of something approaching the totality of himself. The many voices of his play and his emotions ... are all his, spectroscopic fragmentations of a self which willy-nilly speaks in all he writes and which, discovered and released, can speak hereafter in his writing with new richness and vitality."

James Moffett goes further, arguing from anthropological and psychological evidence that extensive experiences in drama are essential to the development of fluency and facility in both oral and written language.

It should be clear that we share this enthusiasm for making drama an integral part of the study of language and literature. But, since we (along with many other teachers) have inherited a profound Calvinistic distrust of enthusiasm (i.e., the belief that you're getting special, personal messages from the Almighty) in any form, we feel bound to devote a long section of this paper to an examination of the reasons why teachers should NOT use drama.

To say it plainly, you do not set out in the English classroom using drama either to make kids healthier or better-adjusted or to express your own creative urges or to train child actors.

An identifiable group of advocates of drama consists of the psychotherapists and the mystics, taken together. (For our present purposes, they may be grouped together, though the mystics would fervently deny they are mystics, and the therapists would gravely resent being categorized with the mystics.)

Be that as it may, both the therapists and the mystics think of what we have been calling drama as something more than a way of teaching, seeing its group techniques as a way to heighten sensitivity, purge the psyche of accumulated inhibitions, create honest loving understanding, and, generally, put everybody back in contact with the Earthmother-collectiveunconscious.

Whether they call what they do improvisation, sensitivity training, encounter therapy, or any of fifty other names, in practice they are practitioners of basically the same approaches we have called dramatic and are concerned with the same classes of phenomena as the drama session.

Whether the practitioners of mystic-therapeutic drama come to it from the theater or the clinic, or from selling aluminum siding and used cars, and whether their approaches are verbal or nonverbal, extensive or intensive, with clothes or without, an essential feature of these group techniques is the intense emotional "high" following upon the violation of certain deeply engrained social taboos and/or the surfacing or revealing or acting out of repressed material.

The blown mind is the beginning of wisdom. The point is to use dramatic techniques to reduce or eliminate differences between the "real" self and the social self that is presented to others.

There is no doubt about the authentic powerfulness of these techniques, and no doubt that they can (in the right hands) facilitate personal growth and (in the wrong hands) really mess people up. It is, in fact, the very powerfulness of these group techniques that must make the teacher very wary of how he uses them (another porcupine quill).

People build up psychic defenses for good reasons. In some cases, breaking down the defenses may indeed clear the way for healthier developments. In other cases, breaking down the defenses may simply destroy the person and force him, in desperation, farther into unreality or into dependence on a stronger other. (There is evidence that groups and workshops with dominant, charismatic leaders are likely to do more harm than good.)

Even trained psychologists make mistakes and hurt people. Teachers obviously, are neither trained diagnosticians nor have enough savvy as psychologists to repair the damage they might inadvertently do in the course of an amateur encounter group.

So don't set out using drama with the idea that you are going to shoot for the Big-Bang, Oceanic-Cataclysmic, Back-to-Eden type of experience. You're a teacher of language, not a doctor or a guru. Recognize that the emotional highs, the free-floating feelings of objectless affection and hyper-elation, that can certainly be induced by a skilled group leader, probably have no place in the school. They cannot be handled in that context.

I've spent so much time insisting on this point because so many teachers make their first acquaintance with drama in a sensitivity group or a workshop; and, if the experience was a good one, they are likely to want to go at once and start using on their students the techniques they have half-learned.

Consider this: participants in a sensitivity group or an improvisational workshop commonly are strangers, who come together voluntarily for the group experience, have it, and then go away, perhaps as better people, perhaps as worse.

A classroom differs from the adult group in two vital ways. First, the participants are there involuntarily, and they cannot withdraw if they are threatened or offended by the demands made upon them. Second, the group will continue in daily interaction for many months, so that the consequences of any mistakes made by the leader or the participants must be lived with and will be compounded. I know of one experimental school that self-destructed, in large part because the faculty was put through sensitivity training at the start of the year. When the inevitable letdown came, the teachers who had so joyously revealed their psychic innards during the group sessions found they could not look one another in the eye, much less work together.

All I am urging is, don't exceed either your powers or your legitimate authority. The student's right to the privacy of his own internal life must not be violated. Students must be allowed to maintain as much distance from the roles they play as they feel the need to maintain. The student is always the best diagnostician in such cases, since he knows when it hurts. (Aren't you glad that no one put Emily Dickinson into sensitivity training to straighten her out?

Let us turn to the second set of objectives you should NOT hold for your own uses of drama — the esthetic or artistic ones. In the hands of a trained and skillful director — the sort of person who may legitimately be said to be professionally engaged in "creative drama" — classroom drama is as much of an art form as modern dance or improvisational theater.

From such drama, participating students can get not only the esthetic and personal satisfactions that are any artist's due, but probably such side benefits as increased self-confidence, gracefulness, verbal and imaginative flexibility and fluency, and heightened appreciation for the arts — all that the drama people claim.

What distinguishes student work under a skilled director from work done in a literature class is that, since the former experience is probably esthetically superior, its benefits are probably proportionately greater. Student work in creative drama is often astonishingly good as artistic performance.

The leaders in the creative-drama movement will tell you that it takes sound training with an excellent teacher and years or even decades of experience to make a good creative-drama director. They will, in fact, tell you that most of the people with both the training and the experience are still not really very good at drama. And they will react to the suggestion that any teacher can become a drama teacher in about the same way that a physician would react to the claim that, after all, anyone can do brain surgery.

And in a way they are right, of course. The English teacher who uses drama for certain specific and legitimate reasons, though he can expect to get better with study and experience and may, in a few cases, find he has a real gift, must reconcile himself to being a Sunday painter, as it were, whom the professionals will never recognize as belonging in their ranks.

English teachers might be well advised to lay off using the term "creative dramatics," just to avoid giving offense to their colleagues in dramatics by implying that the art they have learned over twenty years is really so simple a thing that anyone can master it in his spare time.

All right. You want to use drama, because you are convinced it is a good thing. And you're not setting out to save the world, or to screw heads on better, or to outimprovise Second City, or to cultivate another Marlon Brando. How do you get started?

Read first. Some of the works we list in the last part of this book should become your constant companions for a while, and some of them — Spolin and Barnfield especially — your best references for a long time.

Start modestly, with simpler theater games and language games that do not depart too far at first from familiar classroom procedures. Use the last few minutes of a class period for your first experiments. Concentrate on making the games fun, so the students will look forward to them. Be aware that there is a good possibility that your own inhibitions will be a larger problem than the students' supposed inhibitions.

Summerfield told of a teacher in England who was trying to conduct drama while seated on the podium wearing his academic robes. Didn't work, of course. You have to take off your shoes or your coat and tie and get down and take the chance of making an utter ass of yourself.

Always prepare carefully, and prepare much more than you will possibly need. This will give you confidence and the freedom to cut short any game or exercise which isn't working as you would like it to.

Enroll in a workshop or a class. If you are learning while your students are, things can go much more easily.

Have fun.

Live longer.

"Sir," a man said to the Universe, "I exist!"

"However," replied the Universe, "I don't want you to tell me, baby, I want you to show me!"

PEAK EXPERIENCES
AND THE
SKILL OF WRITING

The color stand out. The red moves quivers like blood the brown, what is it, hair, it must be. Darkness is a frend to it, light an enemy It burns fire, white fire, cold fire, space is its home. Endless time its companey.

The composition reproduced above was written by a high-school student. It is an expression of his feelings — such of them as he could put into words — in looking at Picasso's *Woman with Pears*. Everyone will agree, I think, that it is a very fine and full response to a work of art. Making it must have given the writer a good deal of pleasure and satisfaction. And we know from his teacher's comments that she experienced similar feelings when she first read it, though, no doubt, they came from somewhat different sources.

The intrinsic values in making and teaching ought never be forgotten. But in this case, the likely practical purpose of the work is as interesting as any artistic achievement that can be discovered. To get at this practical side, we need to look at the circumstances in which the work was generated.

One late fall day the teacher gave an in-class writing problem: take the word *freezing*, and in one or two hundred words write an impression of freezing without using either *cold* or *chilly*. To help, the teacher passed out copies of a paper written in the freshman English course at a state university. Considering that provenience, it is interesting to know that the paper was simply a recording of the impressions attending upon the contemplation of a painting. In that, of course, it was like the paper on the Picasso.

After a short while, again intending to be helpful, the teacher began walking around the room and reading what the students were writing. When her perambulation brought her to the writer of our paper, she discovered that he had nothing to show. Probably she was not surprised. If not actually a "discipline problem," the boy seems to be a sort of worrisome distraction to the teacher: "he's tall and *thin*, walks with a cocky swagger and has bulging eyes." Not, it appears, the kind of person who would find much value in so abstract, formal, and writing-ish an assignment as this one.

As it happens we do not know how the teacher responded to the boy's recalcitrance. All we have is her report of what the boy did. For all practical purposes, though, that may be enough.

"That paper you give us was about a pitcher," the boy exclaimed. "If you'd let us write about a pitcher, I could do that."

Such sharp, demanding criticism of a teacher's technique is hardly seemly behavior in anyone, and, indeed, the teacher suggests that the boy's outburst might have been symptomatic of a relationship founded on hostility: " — he's been on my back since September, and I've been at his throat." Yet hostility can hardly have been the sole feeling that held them together. For the boy did not reject the idea of writing in a period the teacher had set aside for it. As a matter of fact, in its essentials the boy's speech in no way took him out of his pupil's role. He seems to have been making a fairly clear and direct appeal to the teacher: "You listen to me, you pay attention to me and what I know and hope about myself, and I'll write you something. I'll do your work — but in my fashion." The boy would write in his own way; but, touchingly, only with his teacher's permission.

If chance had permitted, the boy might also have chosen his own object of attention. As it happened, however, the teacher (we can be happy to know) responded and made the choice for him.

She says that she "flung [her] arm out toward a print of Picasso's *Woman with Pears* and said, 'There's a picture — look at that, and WRITE!' "

And write the boy did. So, if there was hostility between boy and teacher, at least it did not prevent him from accepting her participation in his writing situation. In sum, it looks as if the two of them were supported in their work by some sort of common trust — in their roles, if not in their persons. The point is that the boy did carry through a school writing exercise, in more or less appropriate fashion, as soon as some concessions to his interests had been made. If making sure that all students write, and getting writing from everyone are legitimate desires (objectives) of teachers, then perhaps the shape and content of this little interchange need our study.

The model the boy was given went this way:

Seething, brimming with color, water-fire in motion, the paint breathes life into a stark naked canvas. The pain seeks to stretch all its organ to the utmost length across the white expanse, yet cries in pain with the motion. The earth colors, green and brown, throb in the images as they move forward, carrying all the secrets of that elusive particle — Life. What makes it real and contain the "essence" of life is confusing, and almost rejected by the eye — for what is unreal is now so very tangible to all the senses. The pain breathes, complains. The canvas becomes the universe, the infinity, the unknown. An artist's brush has devastated the hoary canvas and de-

stroyed it of its conformity, which was, in fact, its only uniqueness. The colors must move to survive. The hands in the painting reach forward, toward an end not discernible by my eye, but felt as I view it. Which way is the painting really going; up toward the lights or down toward the earth, where the colors were born? The painting controls my breathing — I must think, feel, experience with the motion of the paint and the color.

I do not for a moment mean to say that the complex of feelings in incidents like this one is part of the material of teaching, of which teachers in some sense should be aware. Of course the boy's speech was an attempt to establish a connection, and one in the heart too; and, of course, in the teacher's response, in addition to her exasperation, were all of her obviously conflicted feelings about him. For both of them the incident must have been valuable for its great and immediate utility. But there is no reason to believe that this teacher knew in any reportable way, or needed to know, what motivated the boy's speech. Nor is it likely that she was much aware of the feelings in her own response — either the hostility that she later called attention to, or those feelings that did not become conscious enough to interpret. The same is true for the boy.

And so, I forego what on other occasions and for other purposes it might be useful or interesting to know or speculate about. The tone of the boy's speech will not be a concern of mine here; whether it was desperate, confident, pleading, hopeful, hopeless, or whatever. Nor am I much interested here in whether the boy intended to gain the teacher's approval, to show what he could do, to show her up, to use her and the class and writing in some intricate inner balancing, or whether he had in mind yet some other end. And the same for the teacher's voice, and the exact form of her outflung arm, especially as it was related to the boy. Of course the "real" cause of the boy's writing was the teacher's outflung arm, her command ("Look in thy heart, and write!"), the college paper as model or stimulus, the picture itself, a combination of all these, or something else entirely.

The colors stand out. The red moves quivers like blood the brown, what is it? hair, it must be. Darkness is ... a friend to it, light an enemy ... burns burns fire, white fire, Cold fire, Space is its home. Endless time its Company.

But the "law of infinite variables" is not quite the king's writ, and surely there may be areas, like thought and speculation, where it doesn't run.

In this incident the important fact is that everything centered on the school exercise of writing a paper. Whatever connection the boy sought or the teacher acknowledged was articulated in terms of a writing assignment. However complicated and numerous the affective components of this interchange, in the end they may all be brought down to the simple concrete exigency of the paper or of a situation in which writing was to occur. And there is no reason or need to go beyond the terms of that situation. We need not ask any more complex or deeper question than, for example, What items in the incident, as reported, allowed or helped the boy to handle his immediate problem, writing a paper?

What counted about the writing situation or the boy's situation as a writer can be found in his speech. That seems to have been, in practical terms, an attempt to legitimize "writing for teacher," to bring the assignment into the boy's own world. This is important. Here is no practice in the rudiments of a skill to be put to use "when you grow up and get a job." What job, in the senses in which the word is used in the school, requires writing about Picasso? Here is no practice in the forms of public argument. What town meeting or business conference (not to mention legislative debate) would be persuaded or even moved by so lyric an effusion as this? Here is not even much evidence of practice on the forms of the standard or prestige dialect, still less of those that define Textbook English.

No. Here is only a boy who briefly brings an assignment into his own world, makes it for a while a part of his own present moment. For ten or fifteen minutes, maybe a few more, he manages to get some sort of command over the impersonal chaos of the classroom, and perhaps over his own life, too. Or to put it less emotively: in and by means of his speech, the boy invested his teacher's assignment with a personal value and utility. He established himself in a role that allowed him to feel that he was writing for his own purpose, at his own direction — in Wordsworth's great phrase, that he was writing from the impulse of his own mind.

What the boy had been asked to do was little more than a trick. The children were given a word (*freezing*), then told to write their impressions of its referent (the act of freezing) without using the two simple words (*cold, chilly*) that, surely, would naturally have occurred to most of them at once. What the boy did was to take this completely pure exercise in writing practice and, by an incredible feat of imagination and indiscipline, set himself a situation in which writing could be, and could result in, a real expression and communication.

And what has he learned? Is that the next question? Well, who knows? Perhaps he has only learned another weapon to use against his teacher. Or perhaps (if his teacher indicated it in some fashion), he has learned no more than that that an adult can be pleased by a cadence like his "Space is its home. Endless time its companey." A trick, that one, to handle his teacher; and since he seems to be a person of some intelligence, no doubt he will go on using the device, for a while anyway, until he senses a negative response in this or another teacher, or is attracted by some other kind of sentence structure. If he should continue with the device, it would then be possible to assert that he had indeed learned something, though nothing of a very high order.

And the teacher? What may she have learned?

But suppose that, with the boy, there is no "follow-up"? Suppose he lapses back into inarticulateness and writing that can be easily disposed of as immature ("below grade level") or illiterate. Or suppose he should, later, turn out to be among the twenty-one percent of 17-year-olds who can't summarize the message given by one of the speakers of an imaginary recorded telephone conversation, or among the twelve percent who can't "write a note thanking their grandmother [sic] for the birthday gift of a puppy."

Or, to return to the writing of response to literature, suppose he fails to cope with an examination question, for example, one like this:

> What is George Eliot's attitude toward the value of work? For help, look at her portrayal of characters such as Dolly, Godfrey, Dunstan, Silas, and any other characters or episodes which you feel are relevant. These characters have several attitudes about work and its necessity and value. What is Eliot trying to say through them?
>
> Use *specific examples* to support your opinions. Refer to particular characters and episodes as they are needed to make your ideas clear. *Evidence* is important for persuasion. You may suggest any theory, so long as you provide supporting evidence.

Or suppose that he is in a class discussion of Richard Wilbur's lovely "Boy at the Window" which you will find on the next page.

His teacher, guide in hand, knows that Wilbur has received two Pulitzer Prizes and that "the poem requires the usual careful attention," even though it has "no particular difficulties." Perhaps the teacher will also want to transmit the idea that the poem is typically modern, not "in the sense of being obscure or weird, but . . . in being tough and unsentimental."

What must be made of the fact that, when asked to write about the poem, this boy may well fail to work out its rhyme scheme, even incorrectly, as in the teacher's guide? What if he can't say "what is meant here by 'enormous moan'?" and can't give the meaning of "bitumen"? (The teacher's guide has, " 'Bitumen' is coal," which it isn't; it "is" only one of

BOY AT THE WINDOW

Seeing the snowman standing all alone
In dusk and cold is more than he can bear.
The small boy weeps to hear the wind prepare
A night of gnashings and enormous moan.
His tearful sight can hardly reach to where
The pale-faced figure with bitumen eyes
Returns him such a god-forsaken stare
As outcast Adam gave to Paradise.
The man of snow is, nonetheless, content,
Having no wish to go inside and die.
Still, he is moved to see the youngster cry.
Though frozen water is his element,
He melts enough to drop from one soft eye
A trickle of the purest rain, a tear
For the child at the bright pane surrounded by
Such warmth, such light, such love, and so much fear.

the elements in bituminous coal. Of course Wilbur uses the word to "mean" *stand for*, the coal making the snowman's eyes; so in a way the guide is right. But imagine our boy had a scientific bent and knew that the extension of the term "bitumen" is such substances as "asphalt, maltha, gilsonite, etc.") Or what if he remembers the rule that the first sentence of a paper can't contain a reference — pronominal, for example — to a word or concept in the title. Will he not then wonder "To whom does the 'he' of the second line refer?" Will he, indeed, answer the questions set by the teacher's guide, or even deal with them?

In sum, what would we have to conclude, if, as seems likely, the incident of the picture should turn out to have no observable consequences for the boy's performance in ordinary classroom situations?

Must we say that the incident had no value because it had no utility?

Must we conclude a lapse in judgment on the part of the teacher, for allowing the boy his own way?

Must we be uneasy because the boy's work does not demonstrate, by means of technical terms, his comprehension of the picture's form or iconography? And must we be concerned because, writing about a picture, the boy wasn't learning to write about literature?

Must we, with William James, say this?

We have of late been hearing much of the philosophy of tenderness in education; "interest" must be assiduously awakened in everything, difficulties must be smoothed away. Soft pedagogies have taken the place of the old steep and rocky path to learning. But from this lukewarm air the bracing oxygen of effort is left out. It is nonsense to suppose that every step in education can be interesting.

Must we?

I don't think so; not really. Even if we don't want to go so far as to say that having a good time is good in itself, surely we can at least try to see that there is a good in the achieved self-discipline that can be recognized, or at least intuited, in such a work as the effusion on the Picasso.

But just here it is necessary to be very careful, and very clear. What counts is the process, not the product — the process and what it helps a child learn about himself and his world.

A child writing is a child doing something that is of value in itself, as a real activity that will and does contribute to his general development. This contribution to development, to growth, is made, first of all, by the process itself — the business, as it were, of creating.

In his great definition of the two imaginations, Coleridge said that the mental functions of the artist or writer's secondary imagination (it "dissolves, diffuses, dissipates, in order to re-create") are themselves worth comparison with the primal act of "all human Perception" (i.e., the discovery of individuality), which is itself "a repetition in the finite mind of the eternal act of creation in the Infinite I AM." And to borrow from Coleridge again, How many conflicting impulses must the boy have ordered by means of making the piece on the Picasso: the feelings he directs toward his teacher; his experience of the painting, of writing, of school; the turmoil of failure, the satisfaction of accomplishment; the awareness of creating — all these, and no doubt many more beyond our ken, can be supposed to have been contained in this process of composing.

We know so little of what might have gone on in that boy's head. We know so little about the process of composition, about how people write. The testimony of authors is diverse, and it is seldom trustworthy.

Try this experiment with your class and with yourself. Ask them to write on the following topic: "The trouble with being open-minded is that your brains might fall out." After ten minutes ask them to stop and try to recapture what went through their heads as they wrote. Do the assignment yourself. Is there any commonality in the process? What relation between process and product is there?

Remember that most good outlines are made up after the essay is written.

There is, of course, a value in the product. Children's writings, it seems clear, must be treated as objects having intrinsic value, or the potentiality thereof. At least in pieces of free writing, which are mostly of an expressive sort, there can be found formal characteristics that seem to warrant the belief that they provided the person who wrote them with the kind of pleasure that ensues upon successful making. Most often, perhaps, those will be single items that have little or no apparent structural relations; but, with some frequency, pleasure-bearing whole structures are to be found.

The color stand out. The red moves quivers like blood the brown, what is it, hair, it must be. Darkness is a frend to it, light an enemy It burns fire, white fire, cold fire, space is its home. Endless time its companey.

Here, for example, the pattern of the boy's "paragraph" seems appropriate to his probable perception of the formal structures in *Woman with Pears.* (It is an early [1909] Cubist or pre-Cubist work.) And when he divided his material between the over-all impression of the picture's shapes and the forces of its colors, the boy was surely demonstrating both his own constructive powers and some degree of awareness of the ways of comprehending paintings. In the second part there is a rather pleasing play with rhythm and parallels, which is especially notable in the cadence. All these surface characteristics of the paper argue that the boy must have some relatively conscious recognition of the properties of the English sentence.

Or at least it can be said that he did, even if accidentally, create a work with formal properties of enough distinction, and distinct enough, to give to an English teacher that sensation which — for lack of some better name — we call an appropriate pleasure. And further, if the boy didn't in any way "know" what he had accomplished, well, then, here there would be just that situation all teachers seek — namely, a growth or learning point. The boy could learn two things. First, he could learn the comparatively trivial facts about parallelism and balance in the sentence. Second, he could also learn, by means of direct experience, the very great value that lies in contemplation of things that are well and truly made. In this case the boy would also learn that something he had made was itself a thing of value, different in degree, not in kind, from the picture that had occasioned it.

Would this not be an educational experience?

A good many teaching successes must depend on the accidents of encounters between teachers and pupils like the one we've been describing. And many teachers have sufficient intuitive sensitivity to carry them off. That is, perhaps, why every so often — once a term, a couple of times a year — most students experience success with a piece of their writing. Some magic or alchemy (so I believe the literature would say) exists in apparently unique situations; the result is a paper that can be judged successful writing (*if that is what is wanted*), as well as the flukishly satisfactory completion of an assignment by a nonwriter.

But teachers need — and children need them to have — something beyond sensitivity to individual cases in their specificity, so they can plan, or make lesson plans. It is not altogether clear how freedom can be planned, but if "planning" can be thought of as "the ability to improvise toward known ends," then I suppose we can derive certain useful principles from the incident of the boy, the teacher, and the picture.

First, the incident partially individualized a whole-class exercise. The boy still had to write along with everyone else, but at least he was doing his own version of the assignment.

Second, the teacher had set no formal or conventional requirements for the appearance of the paper. "There's a picture — look at that, and WRITE," was her only direction.

Third, the stimulus or "motivation" was the complex of actions and feelings that, at that moment, invested a work of art. Note the phrasing. It is purposeful, in hope of preventing any mass recourse to pictures as means of achieving good writing. The Picasso worked, on that day, in that time and place, for that boy. But why it did is a question. And whether it (or some other picture) would work on another day is also a question.

We cannot say it too often. We will not ever be sure — completely *sure* — of what will work for students, even those we know very well (and how many of those are there?), and what will result in experiences that will be valuable to them and also have educational utility. At best, all we can do is be alert for moments when something seems to be happening, and then get out of the way — as this teacher happened to do. Such moments are rare enough; but if we trained ourselves to watch for them and knew that we should, no doubt they would occur more often.

Fourth, the writing was of a personal, expressive, and deeply communicative sort, the outcome of a situation in which impulses toward expression and communication were very strong. The essential fact in the incident was not the kind of writing, but the possibility of using writing for satisfaction of personal ends.

Fifth, the details of the experience, especially the outcome, can all be seen as resulting in "a liberating effect, a freeing or realization of" the urge which is evident in all organic and human life — to expand, become autonomous, develop, mature — the tendency to express and activate all the capacities of the organism, to the extent that such activation enhances the organism or the self.

If you want students to write interestingly and well about literature:

Don't give them writing assignments to accompany each selection.

Don't give them lock-step writing assignments.

Don't judge their writing by the standard of what the professional critic might say about the selection.

Don't grade all their writing as if you were trying to decide whether they should go to hell or heaven.

Don't make everyone in the class do the same assignment.

Do allow the students the right not to write sometimes.

Do let the assignment grow out of the talk you have been having; let it be an extension of the classroom conversation, a setting-in-order of the students' thoughts and impressions.

Do let students modify assignments in the light of their understanding.

Do make clear what you expect from student writing.

Do read and respond to the students' writings as you do to the writing of established authors — somewhat humbly, somewhat tentatively.

Do make writing a process of pleasure, not a punishment.

Only by making writing natural can you allow it to come naturally.

But, it will be said, all this discussion only adds up to what teachers have always known: You get Good Writing when the assignment lets students write about something they're interested in; or, the more real the kind of writing and the more involved the students, the better the pieces of writing they will produce. This principle, which presumably reflects someone's turn away from the faculty psychologies and pedagogical theories of mental discipline that once supported teaching practice, has an attractive appearance of humanity, concern for students, and, of course, realism. And the writing work that it supports, though perhaps not without oddity, still may be preferred to what went on under the older principles.

It is rather hard to imagine any natural situation in which twenty-five or thirty children would organize themselves to write invitations or letters to a governor. But still it cannot be denied that children and adults do, as individuals, write various kinds of social and business correspondence. Obviously, many of them write letters to editors, too. And practicing writing those types of letters may be more valuable, as practice, than doing, say, a paragraph developed by details or comparison and contrast, or composing a three-paragraph expository theme. At least, if they want to, students can imagine situations in which they will need to know the form of a business letter. But who can imagine himself writing a paragraph of cause and effect?

Thurber knew what it was to be a writer of "light pieces running from a thousand to two thousand words," or at least he knew what it meant to Harold Ross, his editor. But do we teachers have any, even the remotest, idea of what students see, feel, and conceive when they hear the word *write*? What does "a paragraph" mean to them, or "a paper," "a theme"? Do they know what we mean when we talk about details and have them practice with Hayakawa's old ladder of abstraction, and then ask them to pick a subject that they know about and that will interest "the reader"? The artificiality and abstractness of the terminology we use to talk about writing are so massive that it is difficult to understand how the dialect can have persisted, if our purpose is, indeed, to help young people "communi-

cate their information and ideas, their imagined conceptions, and their desires and feelings appropriately in situations they meet or may meet — to
speak and write to people."

That is still the best and finest statement that we have of the role of
the composition teacher. I begin to wonder, though, whether it is enough.
For I am more and more aware (and never more so than in writing this
paper) that composition is indeed what Robert Penn Warren has called "a
movement toward meaning."

Robert Penn Warren wrote:

The writer (like any artist) is not a carpenter who builds the chicken coop
according to a blueprint. If the carpenter has a blueprint he knows exactly what
kind of chicken coop will be forthcoming. But the writer, no matter how clear his
idea or strong his intuition of the projected work, can never know what it will
"be" or "mean" until the last word is in place — for every word, every image,
every rhythm participates in the "being," and the "being" is, ultimately, the
"meaning."

This view of writing is not to be found in most textbooks on writing
and rhetoric, for the following reason: We all, no doubt, operate on the
assumption of two kinds of writing; one we think of as artistic or creative,
the other as technical, academic, practical, or what not.

In creative writing, we say, there is some sort of encounter between
the writer and the world, in which the consciousness organizes and
shapes the experience; and the work which results has the form and content it does have because of the interaction of the consciousness and the
world.

In practical writing, we say, the forms (using the word primitively)
are given by some exterior (not to say anterior and superior) authority and
so also, to a degree, the content, which the writer decides about according
to his intuition or knowledge of the audience's capacities or requirements.
No doubt some such distinction would have been called up by Warren, if,
in the 1950s, when he was working on a text on writing, anyone had asked
him and his colleagues to explain their interest in rhetoric. They would

have said then, and perhaps still, that rhetoric is a convenient map for what is, after all, a technology and that — again after all — schooling, if not education, is quite simply a matter of introducing young people to what is known.

Is the opposite of creative writing destructive writing?

We can put aside as too difficult the question of whether writing or the process of composition that Mr. Warren speaks of can in fact be subjected to this neat division. And we can also put aside, for a while, anyway, the question of what rhetoric really maps.

What we can't put aside is the question of whether we can afford to limit the writing of our students to the practical sort, as described above, and to treat the creative sort as a reward for good behavior, something which, since it can't be taught, is not fully a part of schoolwork. We must ask ourselves about the effect that division has on the opportunities for growth in and through using their languages that children may find open to them in schools. That is not at all an easy question to answer, so deep in our consciousness has the division been implanted, indeed so "natural" does it seem. But it is essential that we make the attempt, if we wish to survive.

PROVING THAT YOU'VE
DONE WHAT YOU
SET OUT TO DO
AND THAT IT'S ALL
BEEN WORTH IT

All that we have been talking about in this book may be very nice and very idealistic

BUT

There's a school system out there with

children   parents

state regulations

principals

school boards   department heads

pressure groups   legislatures

colleges   students

administrators

Many of these people don't care whether the students express themselves, whether the students learn how to cope with their environment through one of the many languages at their disposal, whether the students broaden their experiences, broaden their repertoire of responses, whether the students get to know what is in their *heads*.

No, they want the students to get *ahead* — into college, into jobs, into work.

Much of what we have been talking about in this book looks like fun and play; it's not like the old days when we learned all about dates and who wrote what where and when. Shouldn't schools be for working?

But a lot of work can be fun. A person who works and works making a dress or fixing a car engine might enjoy himself just as much as if he were playing football or dancing. Some professional football players and dance instructors look at football and dancing the way some mechanics do at fixing engines or sewing-machine operators do at making dresses — it's something they can't wait to get away from.

Some inventors play with machinery. Scientists often play with ideas. Taxidrivers play with the traffic. Steelmen play. People who enjoy what they are doing and see the challenges in it play with materials, ideas, problems, sometimes even people. Work . . . play . . . it depends how you look at it. Homework, or games to play with when you're at home?

Playing around can be productive. The seeming aimlessness of making a collage may produce in the maker a new understanding of the relations between things, a new sense of his power as an organizer of experience, a new acceptance of the value of order and form.

A seemingly desultory conversation about a play may produce in a student a new understanding about the play's structure, a new sense of the importance of defining terms, a new appreciation of his classmates and their values and perceptions.

There is a potential for human growth in what appears to be play, and this potential is encouraged in a curriculum that fastens on the responses of individuals to what surrounds them. Teachers believe that . . . but are they sure? What about those people who want to know precisely about student achievement in terms of test scores, norms, and percentiles?

"You say it's good for people, but how do I know I can believe you?" That's the sort of question these people ask, and they are justified in asking it. Name your objectives, specify them, prove they're worthy, and prove that they can be attained. That's all these people are asking.

So what's a teacher to do? Sulk? Go back to spelling drills and memorizing dates and places? There's no need to do that. All that we have been talking about so far is certain kinds of performances that we think students can become competent to do. Perhaps they are already competent and don't know it because no one has asked them to demonstrate it.

When we think about the objectives of an English program, perhaps we should think of it as a simple sentence:

SUBJECT	VERB	OBJECT
Students	/will/act out or recite	their version of a story.
Johnny	/can/describe	a poem in his own words.
A student	/may/generalize	about the poet from several of his poems.
A class	/is able to/discriminate	between a play and the images it arouses.
Mary	/should/make an interpretation	of a novel.
That kid in the third row	/might/value	going to the movies over "speed."
The girl who dresses nicely	/can/relate	the metaphor of a play to its meaning.
Most of the class	/should learn to/ express an evaluation	of the books they've been reading.

The subject is usually a student or group of students.

The verb is usually one of the verbs that show action.

The object usually has something to do with what the curriculum is all about — in this case, literature.

In order to prevent oneself from generating endless lists of sentences, one groups the verbs and the objects into separate series. Any verb may, then, intersect with any object; any object may be acted upon by any

	Recognize and recall	Apply knowledge of a work to	Apply knowledge of contextual or critical in evaluation to
Specific literary works	The student will show that he remembers the characters and incidents in a story.	The student will compare and contrast two works as to their mood and meaning.	The student will point to examples of metaphor in a poem.
Contextual and background information	The student will give the dates of composition and background for the poems he has read.	The student will explain how a poem is representative of the period in which it was written.	The student will . . . NO this cell does not make sense!
Critical information	The student will define *metonymy* and *synecdoche*.	The student will show how a play fulfills the definition of tragedy.	Nor does this one!
Responses of readers	The student will show that he can remember how he felt when he saw a film.	The student will show what aspects of the work brought forth a particular response.	The student will point to the metaphors in his description of a poem.

verb. To show this interaction simply, one sets up a grid, using these verbs or *behaviors* and these objects. Here is a grid representative of the spectrum of literature programs in the United States.

Express a response	Re-create or create	Express a preference	To generalize	To value
The student will express in words or some other medium his response to a story.	The student will orally (theatrically) re-present a story he has read.	The student will learn to prefer great literature to inferior literature.	The student will create his own definition of literature.	The student will resist any attempt to censor literature.
The student will express his response to the background information he is given.	The student will dramatize the struggles of a writer he has studied.	The student will show that he prefers writers' works to the lives that have been written.	The student will derive a sense of the relationship of literature to history.	The student will recognize the importance of contextual information and use reference sources.
The student will describe his feelings about a story using the technical terms.	The student will . . . this one's silly!	This one is sillier!	The student will make up his own critical system.	The student will acknowledge the usefulness of terminology in talking about literature.
The student will show what he thinks of other people's responses.	The student will . . . this one's redundant!	This one is not silly, but it's backwards?	The student will typify his response patterns if such exist.	The student will value his responses as being appropriate to him.

BEHAVIORS

a   To recognize or recall.
b   To apply knowledge of a work to something else.
c   To apply knowledge of contextual or critical information.
d   To express a response.
e   To re-create or create.
f   To express a preference.
g   To generalize.
h   To value.

OBJECTS

a   Specific literary works (poems, plays, films, stories, etc.).
b   Contextual and background information (about the work, the author, or the like).
c   Critical information (both terms and theories).
d   Responses of readers.

In choosing among these cells, we limit our attention because we are concerned not with producing literary critics, Ph.D.'s, or English teachers, but with producing people who can respond to a variety of arts freely, who can support a varied cultural life, who will be an active audience for the creative artists of the future, and who will be able to use their imaginations in dealing with the experiences that surround them and with finding solutions for the problems they will face.

   For the response-centered curriculum, then, twelve cells (the ones that are not shaded) emerge as being most important. At the same time, the large grid is not quite adequate to the varieties of responses we have been talking about. If we look again at the objects of attention, we note that we have emphasized two objects.

   Literary works (poems, plays, stories, films, television shows . . .)
   Responses to literary works.

As we have talked about literary works, we have not paid much attention to the background information (the lives of the authors or the historical context of the works). We have not paid much attention to critical terms like *metonymy* and *synecdoche*. We have not paid much attention to various myths or mythic backgrounds.

With respect to behaviors, we find that to *re-create* (or create anew), to *value*, and to *generalize* remain from the first grid. *To express a response*, however, needs to be subdivided for clarity's sake into *to evaluate*, *to interpret*, *to relate*, *to discriminate* (or contrast), and *to describe*.

Which of these behaviors is more important? They are equally important. To describe something without placing some value on what is being described or on the act of describing renders that act meaningless.

Which of the two main objects of attention (the work or the response) is more important? Neither; the work would not count for anything were it not responded to, and the response is nothing without the work.

The grid makes both answers apparent. It shows the interrelation of the various behaviors and objects of attention, and shows their equality with each other as goals of instruction.

The grid, then, represents the general objectives of the program we have set forth. It describes the kinds of things we would like students to be able to do after they have been in the tender care of such a program as ours.

> But these things don't tell us how well
> the students should do at such a program.

Right, but in this program, doing it at all is about as important as being skillful. Enacting his own dramatization of a story he has read is an important action for a student to perform; whether he wins an Academy Award or gets applause from his classmates is less important. It's the participation that counts. For our purposes, then, doing it is most important.

	Re-creates	Values	Generalizes	Evaluates
Work	The student will be able to re-create a piece of writing in some other medium or mode of expression.	The student will be able to demonstrate that he accepts the importance of literature in his personal life and in the world at large.	The student will be able to derive general principles about literature from pieces of writing, and he will be able to apply those principles to other pieces of writing.	The student will be able to state and support his evaluation of a piece of writing.
Response	The student will be able to set forth his response to a piece of writing in some medium or mode of expression.	The student will come to trust and value his own responses to pieces of writing.	The student will derive general principles about how he responds to works.	The student will be able to derive generalizations about the pattern of his responses to pieces of writing and will be able to apply those generalizations to new responses.

> *But just doing it and doing it over and over again doesn't give the students a sense of accomplishment; there must be some proficiency and progress.*

In part that is an apt comment, but only in part. The student moves from selection to selection, and, since each selection produces a unique

Interprets	Relates	Discriminates	Describes
The student will be able to state and support an interpretation of a piece of writing.	The student will be able to relate several elements of a piece of writing to each other and to the whole.	The student will be able to discriminate among pieces of writing, identifying the type of each.	The student will be able to describe a piece of writing in his own terms.

experience as it is met by each student, new kinds of responses occur, each of which calls for a different expression.

At the same time that there is a widening of the student's experiences, there occurs a concentration, as the student compares and contrasts his experiences and derives generalization from them. He comes to develop a style of his own.

He also comes to a sense of sureness in his being able to read and deal with a new story, poem, play, film, or whatever.

To control for this sense of accomplishment, we tend to arrange works in a rough sequence of difficulty. This sequence has four aspects.

I. *Content.* Some works deal with more complex issues than do others, more complex emotions or relationships than do others, experiences more remote from those of most people than do others, or more abstract ideas than do others.

II. *Voice.* Some works are relatively clear in that one is able to determine who is talking and what his attitude towards the subject matter, the audience, or himself is; what his tone is; or what sort of a mood he seems to evoke. Others have a variety of voices, some of which a reader can trust, others of which he cannot.

III. *Language.* Some works use more highly complex syntax; some use many allusions; some build pun upon pun; some are highly metaphoric or imagistic.

IV. *Shape.* Some works use a clearer visual organization than others; some works have more complex sound patterns than others; some works have more complex plot or organization than others.

Using content, voice, language, and shape as rough guides, one can make a curriculum that goes from relatively more simple to relatively more difficult works. Such guides must be rough because works just do not fall into a simple progression from easy to hard. *A Tale of Two Cities* has a complex plot, although it is fairly straightforward in its presentation of Dickens's attitudes. An E. E. Cummings poem might have a simple content but complex language and structure. *Macbeth's* language is harder than that of *The Cherry Orchard*, but it deals with less subtle emotions. A rigidly programmatic curriculum can't be structured; a loosely programmatic curriculum can, particularly if one takes content as the main structuring principle and lets voice, language, and shape modify that structure.

Thus, we can say that achievement in the curriculum is defined as facility and sureness of response to the next selection the student is exposed to.

> *A student has learned to bat if he makes a hit his next time up, not if he remembers how the pitcher looked the last time or what the coach told him.*

> *A student has mastered the process of responding if he responds surely and easily to a new selection, not if he remembers the teacher's lectures on the last selection.*

We prove we can do by doing, not by remembering what we did.

If we prove we can do by doing, <u>the teacher's job is not to devise tests on past performance but to observe and evaluate present performance.</u>

> When we look at present performance, we must observe two things.
> *How well students do what we want them to do.*
> *Whether they will do what we want them to do when they're left to their own devices.*

After all, if you get students to read T. S. Eliot very carefully, finding all the paradoxes and ambiguities and relating them to the mythographic background, but they don't ever read a poem or story again, have you succeeded?

If you get people to read a lot of poetry and go to plays but do so without being able to do much more than grunt, "I like it," have you succeeded?

> We want both competence and interest.
> If we want both, we have to measure our success both ways.
> We have to see whether students will and if students can.

TOOLS FOR SEEING IF THEY WILL

a   a class

b   an observer — the teacher, a teacher's aide, a supervisor, some students.

c   a means of recording what is seen — a videotape or tape recording of the class (this is useful but not necessary).

d   a checklist for recording what is done.

It might simply be a class roster which has a blank after each name for notes about who did what.

It might be a blank form of our grid (p. 186) on which the students' names are placed in the cells which best describe what they do.

It may be a form which shows not only who did what but whom they did it with.

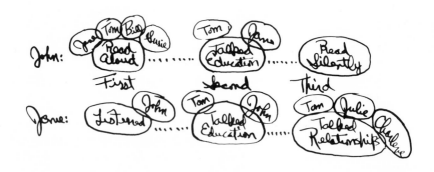

These aren't easy tools to use; it takes practice, but no more practice than it takes to write a good multiple-choice test.

Once you have them down, you can show what students will do in class.

SEEING IF THEY WILL

If, on the first day with a new class, you walk in, give your students ten selections, and say, "Each of you do what he wants to do by way of responding to one selection," odds are that many will want to know what sort of a response *you* want. They may do nothing that first time.

If you walk into class the last week of a year spent with a class, give them ten selections, and say, "Each of you do what he wants to do by way of responding to one selection," odds are that all will do something, but that you cannot fully predict who will do what, and several will respond in ways that might offend you deep down.

They have learned to express their responses freely.

If they show each other what they do, many will comment on the other's responses, and there will be a lively exchange.

They have learned to respect each other's responses and to value their own. They might even show they have learned to generalize, to evaluate, to interpret, to relate, to discriminate, or to describe.

TOOLS FOR SEEING IF THEY CAN

1. A class

2. Some selections and some questions — "Which is better?" "What do these have in common?" "What significance do you find in each of them?" "Make a collage representing your impression of one."

3. A means for students to respond: paper and pencil, a tape recorder, a videotape, film, pictures for collage-making

4. Some criteria to judge by

   a Re-creating ("performing"): Does the student appear to be translating into speech, writing, pantomime, pictures, or some other medium a consistent view of the selection, author, character, mood, action, or meaning? Does the re-creation make sense in terms of the selection (is it possible? plausible? probable?)?

b   Valuing: Does the student state his values clearly and seemingly honestly? Is he simply seeking to please the group or the teacher, or is he being independent?

c   Generalizing: Does the student display an awareness of the relationship between examples and generalizations? Does he avoid the hasty generalization? Does he go too far the other way and never risk a generalization? Is he aware of the tentativeness of generalizations? Does he distinguish between generalizations and prejudices?

d   Evaluating: In stating his evaluation of a selection or of his response, does he establish criteria and then match the selection or the response to the criteria? Or, does he simply say, "It's good because it's good"?

e   Interpreting: Does the student make explicit the context of his interpretation (does he specify that he is looking at a selection from a social rather than a psychological point of view, for example)? Does the student relate as many facets of the selection as possible to the interpretation?

f   Relating: Does the student show the points of commonality between two selections? Does he show the relationship between parts and whole? Does the student avoid the trap of confusing relationship and identity? Does the student note the relationship between seemingly opposed responses to a selection?

g   Discriminating: Does the student show the unique qualities of the selections or parts of selections that are being discriminated? Does the student discriminate between the work of literature and his response to it so that he sees the work as a partial cause of his response?

h   Describing: Does the student make a verifiable description of the work or his response to it? Does his description need more precision?

SEEING IF THEY CAN

When we seek to find out if they will, we cast a net and see what we catch; when we seek to find out if they can, we ask them to hit a target we set up, or we look at what they do and judge them not on whether they do what *we* want but whether they do what they want well.

In that case, we use a criterion, some explication of a good performance. Oh, it does not have to be a rigid definition. After all, we use a lot of criteria when we determine a good meal or a good film; we should be as flexible in judging a student's paper, collage, or improvisation.

There is no reason to make our criterion that which we apply to an essay by a famous critic or a performance by a theatrical group, or even an exquisitely done collage. We can, for instance, do little better than have a recorded class discussion of a selection.

Choose one or two selections that you might think are difficult for the students, give them to half the class and let them talk. Make notes or, better, use a tape or videotape recorder.

As you listen to the class or the recording, make notes about where you think the students might have checked something, where you think a student did a particularly good job picking up on somebody else's ideas, where you can suggest another example, and so forth.

Play back the tape and hand out your "marking" of the discussion. You might also note the group as a whole, and invite the rest of the class to comment. They might pick up places where people were arguing from different premises, or when a person scored a really fine point.

Seeing if they will and seeing if they can — both forms of evaluation: or rest not on finding out what students remember in a passive way but on what processes of thinking, feeling, responding, and imagining they can bring to bear on a new experience.

Both forms of evaluation depend less on the teacher's making up a test than on the teacher's establishing a situation and observing what, in fact, the students do.

Like the curriculum itself, the assessment depends on performance and process. It measures the length of the quills without annoying the porcupine.

That's very fine, but there are all these national tests

Most of those national tests measure a student's ability to use words, to read unfamiliar texts, and to make inferences. All we have set forth should lead to mastery of that kind of test, bad as it may be, and should do so better than a curriculum that is geared to recall, recognition, and application alone.

Besides, the curriculum we advocate seeks to avoid the trap into which earlier curricula fell. In the past, education in literature spent so much time being scientific, being historical, being something else, that it neglected the fact that literature is written for enjoyment and instruction, that it is intended to be read and responded to, not to have term papers written about it or to be the subject of a recitation.

In one school a teacher asked 23 questions on *Macbeth* in fifteen minutes, questions like *What does this word mean? What does the next line mean?* After class she was asked whether the students liked the play. "I don't know; I haven't time."

If a curriculum pays attention only to recitation and term papers about literature, the students may learn to dislike literature, and English, and school, and the mind.

"You've murdered *Hamlet* and *Macbeth*. What more do you want? My Blood?" wrote a student on a national examination.

Literature and the arts exist in the curriculum as a means for students to learn to express their emotions, their thoughts, and their imaginations as they enter into the experiences of the works they read and transliterate those experiences into film, talk, silence, writing, collage, or the like.

Literature and the arts in the curriculum can both free the imagination and help people order their worlds.

This function is served by no other part of the curriculum.

Without freedom of the imagination and personal order there can come a repressive or a revolutionary society.

Such runs the most pragmatic defense of the curriculum we have suggested. It is a curriculum designed to promote individuality, to promote understanding, to promote the imaginative capacity in all parts of our society.

SOURCES

THINGS RELATED TO NEW SOURCES OF LITERARY SELECTIONS

MAD magazine, *Hot Rod,* and others. (What periodicals do kids in high school read?) Keep your eyes on what they read when they read what they want to read.

Whannel, Paddy and Hall, Stuart. *The Popular Arts.* Pantheon, 1965. A good introduction to ways of looking at popular arts.

The Whole Earth Catalogue, especially *Big Rock Candy Mountain,* its educational supplement. Lists educational materials and ideas suitable for all sorts and conditions of people. Portola Institute (alas, going out of business).

AEP Paperback Book Clubs. The Education Center, Columbus, Ohio 43216. For books for teenagers.

Empacher, Marjorie R. and Trickey, Katherine W. "Easy-to-Read Adult Books for Senior High School Students," *English Journal,* LVII (February 1968), 193–195.

"More Sources of Free and Inexpensive Material." *English Journal,* September Issue.

Marlowe, John W. and Hosman, Francis J. "If Someone Can Begin: PEGASUS," *English Journal*, LVII (February 1968), 206–208. Evaluates a program for bringing the live poet face to face with the student.

Divoky, Diane, Ed. *How Old Will You Be in 1984?* Avon, 1969. Collection of articles from high-school "underground" newspapers.

The Drama Review. New York University. A periodical about things theatrical.

Fader, Daniel N. and MacNeill, Elton. *Hooked on Books: Program and Proof*. Berkeley, 1969. Good lists of popular books.

New American Review. New American Library. A paperback quarterly of essays, short fiction, poetry.

The New York Times Book Review. To keep up with new fiction and one or two responses to it.

Paperback Books in Print. R. R. Bowker Co. A periodical index listing thousands of books.

Penguin Books, Inc. See especially their paperback series of modern poets, English and translated into English. African fiction as well.

The Saturday Review. Another source of new titles.

The *MAN* series. Geoffrey Summerfield, Advisory Editor. McDougal, Littell and Co., 1970. Selections by outstanding contemporary writers who really communicate with today's young people.

Geoffrey Summerfield, Ed. *VOICES*. Rand McNally, 1969. "An anthology of poems which are not afraid to face up to the realities of life in today's world."

Stephen Dunning, Ed. *Reflections on a Gift of a Watermelon Pickle*. Scott Foresman, 1967. One of the better poetry anthologies.

_____. *Some Haystacks Don't Even Have a Needle*. Scott Foresman, 1970. Another one.

Helene D. Hutchinson, Ed. *Mixed Bag* (artifacts from the contemporary culture). "The purpose of this book is to excite interest and elicit emotional response by bringing into the classroom the colors and forms of the world outside. Advertisements, buttons, cartoons, photographs, paintings, graffiti, and song lyrics are carefully integrated with provocative written materials such as poems, stories, and essays to provide an idea explosion in a mixed bag."

Dunning, Stephen. " 'I Really Liked It': Short Stories and Taste," English Journal, LVII (May 1968), 670–679.

Church, Bud. "Beat the Street," Media and Methods, March 1968, 14–17. ". . . . the individual nurtured in the street, either the back streets of suburbia or the center streets of the city, can be reached by literature. . . . Our job as English teachers is to find out which literature is relevant for which kids, excluding no one."

Daigon, Arthur and Ronald LaConte. Dig USA. Bantam, 1971. A potpourri of writings, pictures, drawings, about American youth.

Daigon, A. and LaConte, Ronald, "A Tract in which Certain Starting Proposals are made Accompanied by Practical Activities Guaranteed to Generate Pleasurable Teaching Experiences," Media and Methods, January 1971, 29ff. ". . . a call to explore whatever is important or potentially important to young people, using artifacts and documents found anywhere in the environment that somehow bear on what is under study. Such materials will include not only the familiar printed materials associated with English instruction collected in textbooks and paperbacks, but any item printed or pictorial, graphic or tabular, artistic or prosaic, commercial or public, symbolic or discursive, — anything which has the possibility of revealing some facet of what is of concern to learning."

For recordings of literature, get the catalogues of:

Caedmon	Folkways/Scholastic	Spoken Arts
505 Eighth Avenue	906 Sylvan Avenue	59 Locust Ave.
New York, N.Y. 10018	Englewood Cliffs, N.J. 07632	New Rochelle, N.Y. 10801

Repu, Sato, Ed. *This Book Is About Schools.* Pantheon, 1971. "... the kind of book that inspires action, that excites, that makes one say, 'Why don't I try something like that?' "

Terry, Mark. *Teaching for Survival.* Ballantine, 1971. "Offers a descriptive guide for reshaping our attitudes toward environment; it compels us to consider the way we think, act, and use as a totality." Excellent bibliography on all facets of environmental education."

Silberman, Charles. *Crisis in the Classroom.* Random House, 1970. A discussion of the problems and promise in American education.

Frye, Northrop. *The Educated Imagination.* Indiana University Press, 1964. A wisely humane book.

Holbrook, David. *English for the Rejected.* Cambridge University Press, 1965. A British teacher's detailed account of students who talk, write, dramatize, and read.

Dixon, John. *Growth through English.*

Muller, Herbert. *The Uses of English.*

Moffett, James. *A Student-Centered Language Arts Curriculum, Grades K–13.* Houghton Mifflin, 1969. A great step into the world of language as people use it.

This Magazine Is About Schools. The Everdale Press. A quarterly.

Purves, Alan C. "You Can't Teach Hamlet, He's Dead," *English Journal,* LVII (September 1968), 832–836. "We do not start with the text so as to end with a particular response. Rather, we start with the response and see how adequate it is to the poem as a whole and as the sum of its parts."

Daigon, Arthur. "Finding Ithaca," *Media and Methods,* Februry 1969, 32–33 (reprinted from the *Connecticut English Journal,* Fall 1968). "Devotion to the learner's real and possible worlds and to the judicious exploration of each discipline's unique mode of revelation surely leads toward the profession's long-sought Ithacan anchorage."

Rosenblatt, Louise M. *Literature as Exploration*. Noble and Noble, 1968. "Teaching becomes a matter of improving the individual's capacity to evoke meaning from the text by leading him to reflect self-critically on this process. The starting point for growth must be each individual's efforts to marshal his resources and organize a response relevant to the stimulus of the printed page. The teacher's task is to foster fruitful interactions — or, more precisely, transactions — between individual readers and individual literary works." (p. 26.)

Rosenblatt, Louise. "Pattern and Process — A Polemic," *English Journal* (October 1969), 1005–1012.

McLaughlin, Frank. "Teaching — the State of the Art," *Media and Methods*, May 1968. "Every child invents himself. Presumably schools should enhance this process."

McLaughlin, Frank. "A Recipe for Triggering Relevance," *Media and Methods*, January 1969, 22–26. "Learning (unless it is peripheral) won't take place until students are 'engaged' with tasks they feel meaningful. . . ."

Rouse, John. "Lecture Me No Less," *Media and Methods,* February 1967.

Rouse, John. "I Feel So Breakup," *Media and Methods,* May 1969, 31–35. ". . . he will want to talk about the conflicting ideas, read about the experience of others with them, act out in a dramatization the conflicting feelings, and perhaps even write a poem that expresses a new insight or attitude."

Borton, Terry. *Reach, Touch and Teach: Student Concerns and Process Education*. McGraw-Hill, 1970. Summarizes the initial efforts of the Affective Development Project of the Philadelphia schools dealing with urban environments in education. Additional samples of materials from the project can be obtained by writing to the Philadelphia Board of Education, 21st Street, South of the Parkway, Philadelphia, Pa. 19103.

Postman, Neil and Weingartner, Charles. *The Soft Revolution*. Delta, 1971.

Rosenthal, Robert and Lenore Jacobson. *Pygmalion in the Classroom*. Holt, Rinehart & Winston, 1968. Report of a study of the effect of teacher expectation on student performance.

Creber, J. W. Patrick. *Sense and Sensitivity*. University of London Press, 1965. (NCTE).

THINGS RELATED TO THE CLASSROOM AND TALK

Holt, John. *What Do I Do Monday*. Dutton, 1970. "Shows how conditions may be created — by use of art, films, tape-recorders — which foster the child's sense of the wholeness and openness of life."

Kohl, Herbert R. *36 Children*. The New American Library, 1967.

Kohl, Herbert R. *The Open Classroo*m. New York Review-Vintage Book, 1969. Two books that have helped change our thinking education.

Ardrey, Robert. *The Territorial Imperative*. Dell, 1966. Gives a sense of the classroom as space.

Exercise Exchange
A biennial publication for the interchange of classroom ideas among teachers of composition and literature in high schools and colleges — send all manuscripts and letters of inquiry to:

Thomas J. Roberts
EXERCISE EXCHANGE
c/o Department of English
The University of Connecticut
Storrs, Conn. 06268

(hopefully, still in existence)

Kozol, Jonathan. *Death at an Early Age*. Houghton Mifflin, 1967.

Postman, Neil and Weingartner, Charles. *Teaching as a Subversive Activity*. Dell, 1969.

> *Are these now classics?*

McCloskey, Mildred G., Ed. *Teaching Strategies and Classroom Realities.* Prentice-Hall, 1971. "Geared to today's youth, the strategies presented are primarily aimed at involving students significantly in the process of learning." The text is a compilation of short articles by MAT interns from University of California, Berkeley. Good especially for the beginning teacher. (For English classes the following look good — "Improvisational Drama," "Using Collages," "Filmmaking," "Getting the Teacher to Shut-Up.")

Britton, James. *Language and Learning.* University of Miami Press, 1971. A good book on developmental uses of language.

Cross, Janet S. and Nagle, John M. "Teachers Talk Too Much," *English Journal,* LVIII (December 1969), 1362–1365. How to break the habit.

Barnes, Douglas, James Britton, and Harold Rosen. *Language, the Learner and the School.* Penguin, 1970. Helps show how the teacher's talk affects students, tells what student talk might be like.

Dixon, John. "Creative Expression in Great Britain," *English Journal*, LVII (September 1968), 795–802.

Wilkinson, Andrew. "The Concept of Oracy," *English Journal*, LIX (January 1970), 71–77. This British educator writes about the centrality of talk to the teaching of English.

THINGS RELATED TO FILM, TAPE, VIDEO

Wagner, Robert W., and Parker, David L. "A Filmography of Films about Movies and Movie-Making." Eastman Kodak, 1969. Contains titles of some 169 films on the subject of filmmaking plus a comprehensive list of names and addresses of film distributors.

Fischer, Edward. *The Screen Arts: A Guide to Film and Television Appreciation.* Sheed and Ward, 1969. A good introduction to the technicalities of film.

Epple, Ron. "A Great New List of Short Films," *Media and Methods,* March 1971 (available in reprint). ". . . films which involve some degree of

artistry on the part of the filmmaker" — "Many of the films are character-
ized by their source — underground film schools, etc., sources which traditionally reflect less restriction in theme and technique ... many ... cannot
be used indiscriminately by every teacher and every group."

Marcus, Fred H., Ed. *Film from Literature: Contrasts in Media,* 1971.
"Twenty-four illustrations of scenes from movies are contained and a list
of rental sources for 16mm movies is included."

McKowen, Clark and Sparke, William. *It's Only a Movie.* Prentice-Hall,
1971. "Contains poems, short stories, fables, ... all intended to stimulate
thought, to tie the films to the entire culture. ..."

Denby, Robert V. "Film Study in the Secondary School." *English Journal,*
LVIII (November 1969), 1259–1267.

REVIEWS OF DOCUMENTS ABOUT FILM STUDY, COSTS, LISTS OF FILM

Kapple, F. "The Mixed Media — Communication that Puzzles, Excites, and
Involves," *Life,* July 14, 1967, p. 28.

Kuhns, William and Giardino, Thomas. *Behind the Camera.* Pflaum, 1970.
"Basic book for novice filmmakers. Technical instruction followed by a
log kept by a group of Pittsburgh high school students that describe their
every step in planning and producing a 16mm sound film."

Leahy, James and Routt, W. D. *Rediscovering the American Cinema.* Films
Incorporated. "A classic film guide and catalogue combined containing selections of movies from the silent era to early 60's."

Lowndes, Douglas. *Film Making in School.* Watson-Guptill, 1970. A first-
rate practical book on helping students make films.

Miller, Doris. "Adventure in Educational Media: Making Sound Film-
trips," *English Journal,* LVII (February 1968). The need to "rouse from
their apathy students used to big screens and the charm of professional
actors on T.V." led this middle-aged schoolteacher to develop her own

sound filmstrips. This article, a list of 19 practical do's and don'ts is the result of her experience.

Slade, Mark. *Language of Change*. Holt, Rinehart & Winston, 1971. "Study of moving images as a language . . . our new languages, unless they are shaped by personal strivings for human meanings, shape a reality that nobody wants."

Sullivan, Sister Bede, O.S.B. *Movies, Universal Language*. Fides, 1967. "The central theme is a new perspective for the 'verbally oriented' English teachers to become 'visually oriented' as their students already are."

Trohanis, Pascal. "Simultaneously Projected Multiple-Images and Sounds," *Audiovisual Instruction,* January 1971. Using as subject matter environmental ecological education, this article is excellent in presenting a step-by-step procedure for the development of a multimedia presentation.

Youngblood, Gene. *Expanded Cinema*. Dutton, 1970. An introduction to the experimental and avant-garde film by a knowledgeable enthusiast.

Rhetoric of the Movie (series 1s-216). Eastman Kodak (address as above). Six super 8-color films on 50-foot reels and teacher's guide. Using familiar language, this series parallels forms of expression used in verbal communication. Intended for language arts teachers who want to use movies as a form of communication.

The entire November 1969 issue of *Media and Methods* is devoted to films and filmmaking. *Especially:*

> The American Film Institute Education Department. "Books on Film and Filmmaking," 50–53 (an annotated bibliography).
>
> Braverman, Charles. "The World of Kinestasis," 61–62. How to make a film on just about any subject in the world without leaving the classroom.
>
> Carrico, Paul. "Student Filmmaking. Why and How," 41–45. "Students assisted by sensitive teachers have discovered filmmaking as a whole new way of seeing and of telling about the world around them."

Larson, Roger. *A Guide for Film Teachers to Filmmaking by Teenagers.* Cultural Affairs Foundation, n.d.

Pincus, Edward. *Guide to Film Making.* New American Library, 1969.

Carrico, Rev. J. Paul, C.S.C. "Matter and Meaning of Motion Pictures," *English Journal*, LVI (January 1967), 23–37.

Scheuer, Steven, and Culkin, John. *How to Study a Movie.* Dell, 1969.

Schillaci, Anthony and Culkin, John. *Films Deliver: Teaching Creativity with Film*, 1970.

Schreivogel, Paul. *Films in Depth.* George A. Pflaum, 1970. A growing series of guides for students and teachers (see brochure enclosed — I'm hoping to get a firsthand knowledge of these, since the guides do not seem to be the Monarch Notes type, which I fear will be coming out on films.)

Sohn, David. *Film Study and the English Teacher.* Indiana Audio Visual Center, 1968.

Sohn, David A. *Film, the Creative Eye.* George A. Pflaum, 1970. A book that studies 17 short films in fascinating detail. Suggested projects follow each film. Includes extensive interviews with many of the talented people responsible for these films.

Poteet, Howard G. "Film as Language: Its Introduction into a High School Curriculum," *English Journal*, LVII (November 1968), 1182–1186. The author includes a film bibliography for both teachers and students.

Putsch, Hank. "The Why and How of the Young Film Makers Exchange," *Media and Methods*, November 1968, 50–51. Thereafter, appears as a rather regular feature in *MM*.

Putsch, Hank. "Some Thoughts on the Value of Filmmaking," *Media and Methods*, January 1970, 58–59.

Best sources for art films:

Contemporary Films/McGraw-Hill
327 West 41st Street, New York, N.Y. 10036

Pyramid Productions
Box 1048, Santa Monica, California 90306
National Filmboard of Canada
680 Fifth Avenue, New York, N.Y. 10019

Sohn, David. "Films with Few Words," *Media and Methods*, February 1969. Excellent annotated bibliography of outstanding short films for the classroom. A multi-sensory approach to writing, reading, and discussion. "I have intentionally omitted many excellent films that use a lot of dialogue or narrative, or are too long for use in a class period of time. What follows is part of the reel world to help students to observe the real world."

Powell, David J. "Basic Bibliography on Popular Arts: Media Study," NCTE/ERIC.

Searles, John R. "Selected Filmstrips and Recordings for the English Classroom," *English Journal*, LV (December 1966), 1216–1220.

Farrell, Edmund J. "Listen, My Children, and You Shall Read," *English Journal*, LV (January 1966), 39–45+.

Media Mix: A Newsletter about Film, Print and Sound in Education. Eight times a year. October through May. George A. Pflaum, 38 West Fifth Street, Dayton, Ohio 45402.

See: Co-published by George A. Pflaum, Dayton, with Screen Educator's Society, Inc., Chicago. Approaches and methods of top film teachers in the country, gives insights into the when as well as the how of film study.

Film Nut News: A more-or-less monthly for film teachers (distributed gratis) Writer:
Alan G. Oddie, 706 Homewood Avenue, Dayton, Ohio 45406

Film News: the international review of AV materials and equipment. Film News Company, New York, N.Y. Published 8 times a year.

Duncan, Barry. *"What Could Be Worse Than Verse,"* *Media and Methods,* January, 1968, 18–20. Tape-recorder techniques can overcome student aversion to poetry.

Encyclopaedia Britannica Films, Incorporated
1150 Wilmette Avenue, Wilmette, Illinois 60091

FILMS, FILMSTRIPS, AND RECORDINGS

Special catalogs: Films with a Point of View

Language Arts — Learning Resources Catalog

Media Plus Incorporated
60 Riverside Drive
Suite 110
New York, New York 10024

NICEM (National Information Center for Educational Media)
McGraw-Hill Book Company
30 West 42nd Street
New York, N.Y. 10036

What *Books in Print* and *Paperbound Books in Print* have done for print media, NICEM's Index promises to do for 16mm films. Educational media reference volumes eventually hope to publish similar indices in filmstrips, listening tapes, transparencies, programmed materials, disc recordings, etc.

PRIME Catalog
Educators PRIME Information Services, Inc.
278 Plandome Road
Manhasset, New York 11030

A multi-indexed directory of materials and equipment for use in instructional programs.

THINGS TO DO WITH VISUAL LITERACY, COLLAGE, GRAPHICS

Rowland, Kurt. *Looking and Seeing.* Four Volumes. Van Nostrand-Reinhold, 1964. Perhaps the best series on visual perception and patternmaking.

Seitz, William C. *The Art of Assemblage.* Museum of Modern Art. 1961. The best historical introduction to collage and assemblage.

Steichen, Edward. *The Family of Man.* Simon and Schuster, 1956. A classic picture book.

Minor, Ed *Techniques for Producing Visual Instructional Media,* 2nd ed. McGraw-Hill, 1970.

Formanek, Ruth and Swayze, John. "Teachers and Technology: Exploring Visual Literacy," *Audiovisual Instruction,* March 1971.

AECT (Association for Educational Communications and Technology) is becoming more involved in the field of visual literacy: distributor for a wide range of visual literacy materials, including films, sound filmstrips, photo story discovery sets, and slide sets. For titles, curriculum guides, and further information, write Director of Publications, AECT, 1201 16th Street N.W., Washington, D.C. 20036.

Visuals Are a Language. Eastman Kodak Company, Advisor, School and Youth Services, Dept. 841. Eastman Kodak Company. Still-picture arrangement, the vocabulary of visual communication, and relationships between visual and verbal expression are some of the topics treated in the magazine. Students will benefit from reading it if they are studying techniques of observation and expression.

Daigon, Arthur. "Doing It," *Media and Methods,* September 1970, 48–49. "An action-oriented series which attempts to turn 'magazine polemics about what education should be into classroom practice' . . . will give you stimuli . . . and corresponding learning activities that call for student use of sound, visuals, writing and other expressive media."

Holland, John, Ed. *The Way It Is.* Harcourt, Brace & World, 1969. Fifteen boys record with camera and comment what it is to live in Williamsburg, Brooklyn.

Miner, Marilyn E. "Charlie Brown Goes to School," *English Journal* LVIII (November 1969), 1183–1185.

Steele, Pater. "Field Photography," *Media and Methods*, January 1970, 51–54. The world of the camera viewfinder is smaller than most, yet is amazingly effective in learning to observe and express the environment.

Strong, William. "Educating the Senses," *Media and Methods*, January 1971, 26ff. "Has to do with pursuing the connections between the rhythms in life and those expressed in literature, film, and the other arts."

THINGS RELATED TO DRAMA IN THE CLASS

Barnfield, Gabriel. *Creative Drama in the Schools*. Hart, 1969. The classic book on the subject.

Cullum, Albert. *Push Back the Desks*. Citation Press (reviewed in *Media and Methods*, April 1969).

Hoetker, James. *Dramatics and the Teaching of Literature*. NCTE/ERIC, 1969. A best-seller among NCTE publications.

McCalib, Paul T. "Intensifying the Literary Experience through Role Playing," *English Journal*, LVII (January 1968), 41–46.

Moffett, James. *Drama: What Is Happening*.

Pitcole, Marcia. "Black Boy and Role Playing: A Scenario for Reading Success," *English Journal*, LVII (November 1968), 1140–1142.

Simon, Sidney and Marianne P., "Dramatic Improvisation: Path to Discovery," *English Journal*, April, 1965, 323–327.

Spolin, Viola. *Improvisation for the Theater*. Northwestern University Press, 1963. Greatest "hidden" treasury of innovative teaching techniques for environmental education.

Stassen, Marilyn E. "Choral Reading and the English Teacher," *English Journal*, LVIII (March 1969), 436–439.

THINGS RELATED TO WRITING

Moffett, James. *Teaching the Universe of Discourse*. Houghton Mifflin, 1968. A classic on language and writing.

Sohn, David and Leavitt, Hart. *Stop, Look, Write*. Bantam, 1969. "For teachers who wish to emphasize writing in relation to observation . . . contains over one hundred excellent photographs."

Macrorie, Ken. *Uptaught*. Hayden, 1970. A personal statement about students' writing and how it can be made real to the writer.

Sohn, David. *Come to Your Senses*. Scholastic Book Services, 1970. Excellent filmstrip pictorial stimuli program. "Since talk, with its searching, arguing, and speculating, provides by far the best raw material for effective student composition, the program aims above all to promote such talk." Teachers' Guide has an excellent brief, annotated bibliography of books for student use, filmstrip programs, picture sets, and short films without words.

Holbrook, David. *Children Writing: A Sampler for Student Teachers*. Cambridge University Press, 1967.

Leavitt, Hart D. *Writer's Eye*. Bantam, 1969. Uses variety of visuals — photographs, paintings, cartoons, advertisements, sculptures and diagrams, to extend and deepen power of observation developed in *Stop, Look and Write*.

Mueller, Lavonne. "Concrete Poetry: Creative Writing for *All* Students," *English Journal*, LVIII (October 1969), 1053–1056.

Rouse, John. "How to Manufacture Tin Ears," *Media and Methods*, September 1967. Maintains that our usual methods in dealing with the sentences students write have produced not better sentences but a deadening of young people's sensitivity to the force, the color, the rhythms of natural American speech.

Rouse, John. "Use Words Because the Skin Forgets," *Media and Methods*, September 1968. "There is no doubt that children begin their school years with active minds and deep emotional lives, and often with a natural ability to put their experience into language. But soon their tongues thicken and they cease to grow in expressive power. After a few years of lessons in composition — in the 'art of effective communication' — reaching out to others through the written word becomes an impossible task. They are ready to join the inarticulate educated."

Gibson, Walker. *Seeing and Writing*. David McKay, 1959.

Gross, Ronald. *Pop Poems*. Simon and Schuster, 1967. This collection suggests how students themselves may take the language of commerce and present it in new perspectives.

Holbrook, David. *Secret Places*. University of Alabama Press, 1965. A fine statement on the real merits of personal writing.

Britton, James. *Language and Learning*. University of Miami Press, 1971. A good book on developmental uses of language.

Fresh Perspectives in Composition. (Eight filmstrips, three 33 1/3 records, and a teacher's manual.) Eye Gate House. A visual approach to composition covering the following topics: Developing Concrete Details; Revising the Composition; Journal-Keeping for Writers; Sample Journal Entries; Stop Looking and Start Seeing; Tips on Writing the Short Story; Tips on Writing the News Story; and Composition Topics.

Photo-Story Discovery Sets. Consumer Markets Division, Eastman Kodak Company.

Peppermint: The Best from the Scholastic Writing Awards, Junior Division. Edited by Jerome Brondfield. Scholastic Book Services, 1962.

Emig, Janet. "The Composing Processes of Twelfth Graders," *NCTE Research Report No. 13*. National Council of Teachers of English, 1972. A thorough case study of how students write.

THINGS RELATED TO EVALUATION AND PLANNING

Diederich, Paul B. "About Evaluation in Reading?" *English Journal*, LVIII (September 1969).

Grommon, Alfred. "Counciletter: Which Ways Now in the 70's," *College English*, XXXI (May 1970).

Guidelines for the Preparation of Teachers of English. English Journal, LVII (April 1968).

Maxwell, J. and Tovatt, A. *On Writing Behavioral Objectives in English.* NCTE, 1970.

Hook, J. N., Jacobs, Paul, and Crisp Raymond. *What Every English Teacher Should Know.* NCTE, 1970.

Squire, James R. and Applebee, Roger. *High-School English Instruction Today.* Appleton-Century-Crofts, 1967. Reports on the success and failure of high-school programs and gives a model of evaluation.

Bloom, Benjamin S., Hastings, J. Thomas, and Madaus, George. *A Handbook of Summaration and Formative Evaluation of Student Learning.* McGraw-Hill, 1970. A good introduction to writing objectives and testing in many areas. Introduces the teacher to the idea of mastery learning.

MEDIA AND METHODS

Especially the feature *MediaBag* which monthly reviews new materials which are of more than routine interest to learning. Each item bears an Infocard number which corresponds to a number on the Infocard in the back of the magazine. Anyone who wants more information on a particular item can check the number on the card and mail it postage-free to *Media and Methods* (useful for films, books, paperbacks, filmstrips, recordings).

RESOURCES

ABSTRACTS OF ENGLISH STUDIES

This magazine summarizes numerous monographs and scholarly articles from more than 1100 journals in the subject areas of literature (by period and genre), in general studies and language (history, linguistics, Celtic, etc.), English and American, and world literature in English. Journals searched include many outside the normal scrutiny of English scholars.

Edited by John B. Shipley, University of Illinois at Chicago Circle. Published 10 times a year (September through June); $7.00 yearly; 3 years, $18.50 for individuals. Institutional rates, $12.00 per year ($33.00 for 3 years). Not available at combination rates. Annual indexes, ordered by year (1958-present), $1.00 each; $1.50 for institutions.

ELEMENTARY ENGLISH

Devoted to encourage better teaching in the elementary language arts, this magazine contains practical, lively articles on reading, grammer, spelling, creative writing, and children's authors, as well as special columns of book reviews of both children's and professional books, audiovisual developments, and news of the profession.

Edited by Iris Tiedt, University of Santa Clara. Published October through May. Included with membership in the Elementary Section of the National Council of Teachers of English (annual dues, $12.00; 3 years, $31.50).

COLLEGE ENGLISH

Editor Richard Ohmann and Associate Editor W. B. Coley, Wesleyan University, Connecticut, select from nearly a thousand manuscripts submitted each year articles on the working concepts of criticism; the nature of critical and scholarly reasoning; the structure of the field; relevant work in other fields; curriculum, pedagogy, and educational theory; practical affairs in the profession; and scholarly books, textbooks, and journals. (*College English* no longer publishes critical articles or explications, except those which have a quite general significance.) Also included: a "Comment and Rebuttal" section and poems. Poetry editor: Susan McAllester.

Published October through May. Included with membership in the College Section of the National Council of Teachers of English (annual dues, $12.00; 3 years, $31.50).

COLLEGE COMPOSITION AND COMMUNICATION

This quarterly magazine features articles on college writing; a typical issue might contain studies of semantics, the teaching and analysis of style, preparing junior college teachers, pidgins, prewriting, film as a method of teaching composition, and an annotated bibliography of heuristics. "Counter statement," a regular feature, presents comment and rebuttal. "Staffroom Interchange" collects short papers on subjects of current interest.

Edited by William Irmscher, University of Washington. Included with membership in the Conference on College Composition and Communication (annual dues, $3.00, with membership in the National Council of Teachers of English a prerequisite, $12.00 a year). Subscription per year to libraries, $3.00; 3 years, $8.00.

ENGLISH EDUCATION

Short, incisive articles on problems related to the preparation of English teachers are included in this new Journal of the Conference on English Education. Editor Oscar M. Haugh, University of Kansas, selects material of interest to members of English education departments and others who prepare English teachers, to supervisors, and to those engaged in curriculm preparation.

Published October, February, and May. Annual dues for CEE, including subscription to *English Education*, $5.00; 3 years, $15.00, with membership in the National Council of Teachers of English a prerequisite. Institutional subscription, $5.00.

RESEARCH IN THE TEACHING OF ENGLISH

Editor Richard Braddock, University of Iowa, and Associate Editor Nathan S. Blount, University of Wisconsin, present articles on new research and a continuous bibliography of recent research in English education. Subjects include language development, reading, writing, attempts to measure quality of response to literature, and other problems of English teaching at all levels. Each issue features a "roundtable review" on a recent report of research and "notes and comment" about recent developments relevant to research in the teaching of English. 1971 EDPRESS All-American Winner.

Published spring and fall. Three-year subscription (6 issues), $6.00; annual subscription (2 issues), $3.00.

ENGLISH JOURNAL

Addressed to teachers of secondary English, *English Journal* brings together articles on language, literature, and composition, ranging in subject from *Beowulf* through *Easy Rider* and the *Dictionary of American Regional English* to surveys of research. Occasionally a special issue presents scholarly appraisals of major literary works or a study of important trends in teaching of English. Columns include "Professional Publications," reviews; "Book Marks," reviews of junior-senior high fiction and nonfiction; "This World of English," pertinent quotes from other journals.

Edited by Richard S. Alm, University of Hawaii. Published September through May. Included with membership in the Secondary Section of the National Council of Teachers of English (annual dues, $12.00; 3 years, $31.50).